Eve Crawford

I Paint Gophers!

Eve Crawford

D1714858

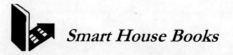

Smart House Books

Smart House Books
Toronto, On.
www.smarthousebooks.com

Book Layout © 2018 Smart House Books
Cover design by Aaron Rachel Brown
Cover art by Sheila Crawford
Edited by Heidi von Palleske

ISBN 978-1-988980-02-7

For my father, who was a master storyteller

And for my mother, who was the story.

And for my two sons.

You are my heart and soul.

Table of Contents

PART I

Bedlam Ridge

The four of us

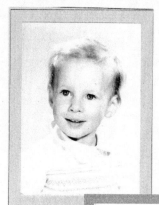

The Dying Swan

Goldie and me

Mr. C

Bedlam Ridge

There were four of us. We were known as the Crawford girls. Dr. Dick Douglas, a friend of my parents, delivered us all. When the youngest, Marti - who was supposed to be Martin - was born, Dr. Douglas, from behind his white mask, intoned to his silent staff, "Poor George." George is my dad.

Although our family lived in Calgary, we spent our summers on a small farm outside the city, where we rode our horses, played in the wading pool and, in general, fought from morning 'til night.

In the mid-fifties, all four of us got pneumonia. It was the cusp of the discovery of the polio vaccine, and our parents, all parents for that matter, were terrified when any of their children came down with a cough. Luckily, none of us got polio. My parents were so relieved that they decided to take us all to the newly opened Disneyland for a celebratory/recuperative trip.

It seemed like a good idea.

But let's take a look at this. We ranged in age from three-year-old Marti, to an eyeball-rolling thirteen-year-old, Sharon. In between were eight-year-old Suzie and five-year-old me, who punched each other out on a regular basis.

So, on a warm July day, Mom and Dad, four daughters in tow, boarded the train in Calgary for the first leg of our trip – a 24-hour ride through the Rockies to Vancouver. When we reached Banff, Dad beseeched Marti and me to look at the view, but we were too engrossed in our comic books to notice the splendid and very *costly* mountain vistas rolling by our window. Dad must have assumed Suzie and Sharon were under Mom's watchful eye. As it happened, that was not the case. Sharon, too embarrassed to be seen with any of us, was just that – not seen. Meanwhile, Suzie was trailing after a handsome eighteen-year-old Mexican porter who frequently kissed her hand and told her that if she was ten years older, he'd marry her. When she wasn't helping him make up the beds, she hung out in the caboose with all the other porters, listening as they told jokes and smoked cigars. I don't know where Mom was. In the bar car medicating?

When we reached Vancouver, we boarded the ferry to Seattle. At this point, it became apparent to Mom and Dad that recuperation, theirs at least, was a non-starter, which perhaps is why they assigned thirteen-year-old Sharon to watch over us while they "took a break." Sharon quickly tired of her babysitting gig, so she dragged Suzie, Marti and me in search of our parents. We spied them through the large window of the ferry's bar. Kids were not allowed entrance, so Suzie and I made pig noses on the glass to get Mom and Dad's attention. They didn't see us - or pretended not to. But the patrons by the window did. They thought we were absolutely hilarious. We weren't *their* children.

It was then that panic-filled screams erupted from the passengers on deck. Marti, whom we assumed had been toddling along behind us, was balancing precariously by her mid-section on the ferry's railing. Giggling in delight, she was flapping her arms in an attempt to take flight. She was a hair's breadth from plunging into the ocean below when a woman lunged forward to grab her from certain death. Thwarted in her *look, I'm a birdie* endeavor, Marti threw a full-on tantrum. The lady, clutching her tight, asked us where our parents were. We dutifully guided her to the bar.

I can't remember whether Mom and Dad were shocked or even embarrassed because, due to all the excitement, I had a full-on asthma attack. My medication was in a suitcase at the bottom of a massive pile of luggage in the hold of the boat. Dad and a steward rushed down to dig it out, but the guy balked when he saw the enormity of the task at hand.

"How are we going to find it in all that stuff?" he protested.

"There is a bottle of Scotch in that bag for whoever finds it first!" barked Dad.

Scotch was my father's solution to most of life's problems and continued to be until his death at ninety.

The next day, we lined up at the Seattle airport to board the plane for Los Angeles. Mom, a basket case when it came to flying, was in urgent need of the cigarettes and gin that flowed freely on airplanes in those days. But first she needed to keep Marti and me busy during the flight, so, at the last minute, she dashed to the airport kiosk where she made the perfectly sensible decision to purchase two sets of cap guns, complete with holsters and sheriffs' badges. It worked a charm. As Dad tended to Sharon and Suzie, Mom happily smoked and drank martinis, while Marti and I ran up and down the aisle shooting the passengers who, to our shrieking delight, feigned agonized and prolonged deaths each time a sulfurous cap exploded in their faces. And why not? There were no movies on planes in those days. And bonus - we weren't *their* children.

Oddly, I have no memory of Disneyland whatsoever. But I do remember our trip to Laguna Beach. Dad rented a blue convertible. Sharon, in sullen silence, sat in the front with Mom and Dad. Marti, Suzie and I were in the back seat, and, when Suzie and I weren't having a slugfest, we yelled at Dad to put the top, "Up, down, up, down!" Marti quietly busied herself with one of those fake steering wheels that let her think she was driving. It occurs to me now that she was the only one who had any control at all.

At Laguna Beach, we checked into *The Pink Pony* motel. Located at the top of a steep road off the freeway, it had a large pink plywood sign in the shape of a pony planted at the edge of the cliff. Soon after check-in, we heard Suzie screaming outside our motel room and ran out to see what was going on. Marti, her little hands growing white as they clutched onto the plywood, was dangling over the freeway! She had slipped surveillance again and, loving horses, had climbed up to go for a ride. Mom got to her just in time.

After we calmed down and settled in, Dad took us to a restaurant where, once we placed our orders, we all started to fight.

He blew up. "Ok, everyone up! We're leaving!"

"But we haven't eaten!" we whined.

He motioned for the waitress, paid the bill, then ordered us to file out of the restaurant. As we passed the hostess station, another family entered with two little girls who wore matching pink, fluffy dresses. They smiled sweetly at the hostess, then curtsied! *Show offs*, I grumbled hungrily. Years later, Suzie told me how much she envied those girls at the time; how much she wanted to be part of that *normal* family.

The next day at the beach, Dad went for a swim. His jangled nerves, no doubt, craved the healing sun and ocean. Most of all, they craved the blissful silence that comes when submerged under water. Sharon, sitting on her towel fifty yards down the busy beach, slathered herself with Bain de Soleil zero protection lotion and pretended she was eighteen. Suzie, Marti and I were building a sandcastle with newly purchased buckets and shovels. Mom, mystery in hand, glanced up at us every time she flipped a page. She must have been engrossed in a particularly riveting section when Marti decided to run over to the water's edge to fill her bucket. She looked up just in time to see a giant wave hit her daughter and suck her out to sea. People nearby plunged into the surf to look for her. It was a miracle that Dad, out on his swim, saw a little leg go by and grabbed it. Only when he struggled ashore did he discover it was – guess who?

A word about Marti. As the last and least supervised of us four girls, she was, by far, the quietest. In fact, she didn't speak until she was two. Not one syllable. Mom and Dad were worried of course, but too exhausted to do anything about it.

At the time, Dad was involved in Calgary's nascent oil industry and had to travel frequently to meet with investors in New York. Mom was left with the four of us and, no doubt, relieved that at least one of us kept her mouth shut. None of us liked it when Dad travelled. Mom got grouchy and depressed, and we were subjected to really weird babysitters. One in particular was a foul-tempered Scotswoman called

Margaret who had terrible asthma, and when she wasn't screaming at us kids, coughed and hawked goobers into the kitchen sink. When we were sick, she would heat up milk, stir in a couple of shots of rye whiskey then stand over us, hands on hips, until we finished it. Marti and I hated Margaret, and our happiest day of the week was Friday, when Mom drove her home for the weekend.

So, needless to say, every time Dad packed his bags, our hearts sank.

On one such occasion, he rushed home from work, told Mom there was an emergency, and that he had to fly out that night. He quickly packed a suitcase, left it on the bed, then went downstairs to join Mom for a drink before his taxi arrived.

Now Marti was quiet but, as has already been established, she was busy. While Mom and Dad chatted in the living room, Marti wandered into their darkened bedroom and stood on tiptoe to see what was in the open suitcase. *What sad looking stuff Daddy had packed.* She would cheer him up. So, she removed his clothes and replaced them with all her dolls' dresses including several pairs of frilly dolly underpants. She closed the suitcase then left the room, happy that she could bring some fun into Daddy's life.

Fourteen hours later – planes took a lot longer in the fifties – Dad met with two investors from Lehman Brothers in his New York hotel room. As he dispensed his expert legal advice, he absently tossed the contents of his suitcase on the bed. As he held his hand up to emphasize a particularly salient point, he noticed the men were gaping. He was clutching a pair of frilly doll's panties.

"I can explain!" he blurted.

But the expression on their faces said, "Sure you can buddy!"

Shortly after Marti's second birthday, Mom and Dad planned a trip to London. Dad hadn't been there since the war, and Mom hadn't been at all. They had hired an Irish babysitter with the unlikely name of Dodo Murphy to look after us. As I watched my parents pack, I felt a queasy feeling settle under my ribs. Marti knew what packed bags meant too and silently viewed the proceedings with furrowed brow. She had just come through a bout of chickenpox but was well on the road to recovery, so my parents had made the decision that it would be ok to press on with their trip. I knew this, because I regularly sat at the top of the stairs and eavesdropped on their drink-before-dinner conversations.

When they were ready to go, Dodo picked up Marti so Mom and Dad could kiss her goodbye. But as Dad leaned forward, she twisted her head away and buried it in Dodo's shoulder. Then she looked up at him and, with a scowl, uttered the first words of her life.

"If you never have a fwend in da wide, wide woild, you've only yourself to blame."

Marti could talk alright, but only when she had something to say.

When she started school, she was tested and found to be of genius IQ. It was something she never flaunted. It manifested itself in the singular focus she brought to everything she did – such as climbing boat railings, mounting cliff's edge, plywood horses, or filling up her water bucket courtesy of rogue waves.

Which brings me back to the beach and her third brush with death.

After Dad had slapped Marti's back to expel a pint of Pacific Ocean, he and Mom packed us all into the convertible. It was on the steep drive up to the Pink Pony that Dad collapsed over the steering wheel. Mom stuck her foot over to slam on the brake, pulled on the emergency, then exchanged positions with him to get us safely up the hill. She herded us all into one bedroom, got Dad in the other, then called the motel desk.

A doctor quickly arrived to check Dad for signs of a heart attack or stroke. His heart rate was high, but of even greater concern to the doc was that he seemed unable to talk. He had been completely mute since his collapse. But the doctor, a man from Montreal, was patient, and perhaps because he *was* a man, Dad finally managed to stammer, "It all started when I brought my wife and four daughters to California for a holiday."

The doctor held up his hand and said gently, "Say no more, Mr. Crawford. I once drove my wife and four daughters from Montreal to Los Angeles. All I can say to you is this: Go home. Now."

And we did.

Dad did not speak another word until we got back to the farm.

For the rest of the summer, he spent much of his time in the garden, and in between pasting wads of mud over his multiple bee stings, he chopped up our large poppy bed, soothed by the chugging of the rototiller that drowned out all noise of his offspring.

It was on one such summer's day that Dad decided to paint a sign to place on a pole marking the entrance to our farm. Our property was at the top of a small ridge that looked over rolling fields beyond. But he couldn't think of a name to capture the essence of the place.

Enter Doctor Douglas. Remember him? The man who delivered us all? Who better to describe us? He was the first person to welcome each of us into the world.

The day he came up with the name, Dr. Douglas was recuperating from some vile infection he had contracted at the hospital. Mom and Dad invited him to spend a quiet day with us in the country. He probably had some soft-focused vision of himself bundled in blankets, breathing in the sweet country air, sipping cups of tea brought to him by my thoughtful mom while he watched George and Sheila's four little girls, *his* little girls, frolic in the sprinkler, ride their ponies and play with their paper dolls.

I don't know why he left early. It was a day like any other day.

I was playing quietly with my paper dolls. Marti, all clothing discarded in the raspberry patch, returned from her naked jaunt down the hill followed by the four Gunderson boys. Suzie decided to make Dr. Douglas feel better by donning Dad's suit jacket and fedora and lip-synching Tennessee Ernie Ford's "Sixteen Tons, Whaddaya Get? Another Day Older and Deeper in Debt." That was before she chased Sharon down the field with the hatchet she had used to chop her way out of the barn, when Sharon, refusing to play with her, had locked her in the tack room. Sharon took refuge inside the pick-up truck that was parked at the end of the field by the pond, locked the doors and leaned on the horn, bringing Mom to the rescue. Dad couldn't hear anything over the roar of the rototiller.

Later, Suzie tried to make up for her little lapse by helping Mom prepare dinner. I think it was when she retrieved the horse syringe from the medical kit, gave it a quick wipe on the seat of her overalls, then used it to inject mint juice into the lamb, that Dr. Douglas said he really wasn't hungry and thought he better be heading home.

It must have been Suzie. After all, Suzie was his goddaughter. Maybe he went home to rethink this commitment.

As he staggered off the porch, Dr. Douglas passed Dad who was sitting on a boulder at the edge of the poppy bed. He had started to paint the sign.

"What do you think Dick? What should we call it?"

Dr. Douglas collapsed his gigantic frame into his Studebaker. He slammed the door, gathered what was left of his strength, rolled down the window and bellowed, "Bedlam Ridge!"

Then he gunned his car down the gravel hill and vanished in a cloud of dust.

Mr. C. and Me

As the third in a line-up of four girls, I lived for many years with the uneasy suspicion that my parents considered me somewhat disposable. Evidence of this came in the nature of the horses I was given to ride.

Horses were a central focus of our family life. The first time I was thrown aboard one, I was in diapers. There is a picture of me, erect and serious, clutching the mane of a sleek grey mare. My mother stands six feet away, holding loosely onto the reins, gazing distractedly into the middle distance. If I fell off, she couldn't possibly have caught me.

The horse, Pepper, was full-grown. That's what my dad thought anyway. She was the first horse he bought, and he did so without consultation. Not a good idea. Dad didn't have a clue about horses. He was good at basketball and badminton and knew about dogs, but the horse department was strictly Mom's area of expertise. As it turned out, this grey mare was not full-grown, as Dad had assumed, but a two-year-old Percheron who soon expanded in all directions to become a massive draught horse, the kind used to pull heavy loads – like beer wagons.

Since no one in the family wanted Pepper after she filled out (my two older sisters got ponies), she was declared *my* horse. By then I was five. I guess my parents decided I was old enough to handle her. They would throw me up on Pepper's broad back, hand me the rope to her halter, which I would grab along with a chunk of her thick grey mane, and send the two of us off for a jaunt around the riding ring.

The trouble was the "ring" wasn't fenced in. It was a well-worn circular path at the top of a steep hill that led down to the oat bin. Pepper would do a perfunctory trot around the circle with me bouncing high in the air, legs in split formation, then, at the end of one rotation, veer off down the hill at a fast trot coming to a lurching stop at the oat shed. There, she would nose open the door, stick in her massive head and feast.

After the Pepper purchase, Dad consulted on all matters horsey with Llewellyn (Llew) Chambers. Mr. Chambers was a crusty Welshman with fierce blue eyes under bushy brows. His go-to attire was a white shirt, baggy tan pants and a crumpled, stained Fedora that he wore squashed on his head. He always had a cigar jammed in the corner of his mouth. Before coming to Canada, he had fox-hunted in England and Wales and his renowned eye for horses landed him a job importing polo ponies for American diplomat Averell Harriman. A real estate agent by trade, his passion, his gift, was his love and knowledge of the horse.

It was Mr. Chambers who found Goldie, a chestnut pony that Dad presented to me on my eighth birthday. I was overjoyed. At last, something I could call my very own. Not someone else's reject like the double bubble chewing gum my older sister Suzie gave me after *she* had worked it over for hours.

Mr. and Mrs. Chambers offered to stable Goldie at their small acreage on the outskirts of Calgary. Mom drove me there every day after school, where, under Mr. Chamber's stern tutelage, I learned to ride and, more importantly, care for my horse. Those days are golden in memory. The Chambers were childless, and when I was there, I had their full attention – a rare commodity for me.

Mr. C., as I learned to call him, was patient but strict. He taught me how to move around a horse, always talking, always touching the animal so it knew where I was at all times. I learned how to groom, tie, saddle, and bridle Goldie. In the riding ring – yes, it had a fence – he taught me the value of gentle hands on the reins, of sitting tall in the saddle, of squeezing my legs to push the horse onto the bit. After the ride, I cleaned her hooves, brushed down the sweat marks until her coat was a burnished gold, then gave her water *before* the oats so her stomach wouldn't swell.

Next came the best part. Mr. C. and I would walk back to the house, wash up and then join Mrs. Chambers in their living room. As I sat in the big chintz armchair in my hole-ridden corduroy overalls, I felt like a queen. And I was treated like one. Mrs. Chambers served tea and crumpets from a gleaming silver tea service she had brought with her from England. Her eyes were the same blue as the Dresden cups.

"Tea, Evie?"

"Yes please."

"Milk Evie?"

"Yes please Mrs. Chambers."

"Sugar, Evie?"

"Yes please!"

Her silver tongs poised above the sugar bowl, she asked solemnly, "How many?"

"Three please."

Then, with deliberate grace, she dropped three lumps into the cup and presented it to me. Two crumpets, three cups of tea and nine lumps of sugar later, my mother picked me up. I was in a state of bliss.

I soon started riding Goldie in horse shows. Most were gymkhanas – equestrian events for kids that involved a lot of skill-testing games. One in particular, the sack race, involved galloping our horses to the far end of the ring where we would dismount, get into a sack, then hop back to the finish line, leading our mounts. That we lived astounds me. Ribbons were given to the winners: red for first, blue for second and white for third. The losers were also given ribbons. This was the beginning of the self-esteem movement, where every child must feel like a winner. I hated those ribbons, and I got a lot of them. They didn't fool me or any other kid. They were green and screamed in big gold letters – NON-PREMIUM.

As I advanced to the more serious shows, I competed in equitation, a class that judged riding skills. The judge stood in the center of the ring with the ringmaster who called out commands to walk, trot and canter. Eventually, the riders were instructed to line up in the centre of the ring where we waited, hearts pounding, to hear if our name would be called to receive a ribbon. Mine rarely was.

But worse than losing was this: if Mr. C. saw me doing something wrong, he would cup his hands around his mouth and let out an ear-splitting howl, one that he used to gather the hounds in his fox-hunting days.

"Hawooooh hah! Evie! Take hold of that horse!"

Mortified, I could hear people in the grandstand hiss, "Shhhh."

But public disapproval was of no consequence to Mr. C. My skill as a rider was.

By the time I was eleven, I had outgrown Goldie. So, Mr. Chambers gave me one of his horses, Nipper. A fat, mid-sized Appaloosa, she had a habit of going lame every time he trained her for a show. It turned out that she had been faking it for years, because once she was put out to pasture, her limp miraculously disappeared, and it was with smug delight that she grazed greedily on the rich summer grass, her girth expanding with each succeeding day.

To her dismay, I started to ride her. Well, I tried. But every time I swung onto her back, she turned her head and nipped my bum. I would dismount and put her back in the corral.

"I don't like you Nipper. No treat for you!"

Then, I would stomp back to the house and grouse to Mom, "I hate Nipper! I just hate her!"

Did I mention I was eleven?

Nipper, however, was a real foodie and soon figured out that to receive her treat, she had to stop nipping. As soon as she did, we became new best friends.

I never showed Nipper, but I did take her to an event that the horsey set in Calgary loved – the fake foxhunt. No fox, no hounds. Just five miles of countryside with jumps set up along the course. All the riders wore jodhpurs, riding jackets, and crash helmets and pretended to be British. We were divided into three groups according to experience: advanced, intermediate and beginner. A hunting horn sounded at ten-minute intervals. My Mom took off with the advanced group on her thoroughbred, Rodney, who had recently been retired from the racetrack because he always came in last.

I was in the intermediates. When our horn sounded, I released Nipper's reins. Well! In spite of her aversion to horse shows, Nipper, it turned out, was a madly competitive little mare. Ears flat back, she bolted forth. Weaving her way through the other horses, she nipped the hind end of anyone in her way, then farted a furious farewell as we sped past.

A quick aside about Nipper's farts. They ruined my dating life.

In my late teens, I asked a guy out to the ranch for a ride. I packed a lunch and a thermos of coffee with the romantic vision of the two of us having a picnic at the top of a ridge that overlooked the stunning Rocky Mountains. I rode Nipper, because she was too bitchy to foist on anyone else. My date, on one of the better-behaved horses, followed behind. All went well, until we reached the steep climb to the ridge. Nipper hated exertion, so, to get the climb over as soon as possible, she galloped to the top where, heaving and sweating, she came to a lurching stop. The problem was, in order to propel herself up the hill, she let out a steady stream of grass-fueled farts right in my date's face! At first, I pretended, as one does with farts, that they weren't happening, but eventually, out of sheer decency, I tossed a "Sorry, sorry!" over my shoulder.

A picnic? I don't think so. A kiss? Please!

After I grew too tall for Nipper, Mom decided to give me Rodney. Gee, thanks Mom! Maybe it was his three-year losing streak on the racetrack, but Rodney seemed to have given up on life in general. Forget racing, he *walked* in slow motion, his head drooping so close to the ground that, when he lifted it, his nose was covered in dust. It was embarrassing. It was as if he were signaling to the world that he was receiving regular beatings at the hands of the Crawford family. I worked on him in the ring, tried to cheer him up, to let him know that life *was* worth living. I spent hours trying to get him to lift his head, to tuck in his nose, to show the world what a fine specimen of a thoroughbred he was. All to no avail.

Why I entered him in a local horse show, I have no idea. But there we were on a fall afternoon: Rodney slumped forlornly like Eeyore in *Winnie the Pooh*. As I was saddling him up for the hacking class, Mr. Chambers came by to say hello. He studied Rodney for a moment then, cigar bobbing up and down in the corner of his mouth, declared, "That horse looks like the 'Retreat from Moscow.'"

Mom, who was in the backseat of our car sorting dirty laundry, poked her head out the window.

"Yes, yes! That's exactly what he looks like."

I knew nothing about the retreat from Moscow so she gave me the Cole's notes version. War of 1812. Napoleon is suckered deep into Russia only to find himself having to retreat from Moscow during the bitter Russian winter. The men and horses, not picked off by murderous Cossacks or hypothermia, drag themselves back to France.

Mom's eyes widened. "I know, Eve. Forget the hacking class. Let's enter the two of you in the costume class. You can go as 'The Retreat from Moscow.'"

"I don't have a costume."

Mom held up a handful of dirty laundry. "Yes you do."

That is how I found myself slumped aboard Rodney, wearing

17

Dad's pajamas, a shirt for a sling, with a dish towel (covered in Ketchup from the concession stand) wrapped around my "bloodied" head. I entered the ring riding barefoot and bareback, a wounded, starving French soldier, on the retreat from Moscow.

Competition was fierce. The mothers of the other kids had spent the summer constructing their costumes. A headless horseman – head tucked under his arm – looked through a mesh opening of a *papier mâché* neck painted with blood drippings. There was Lady Godiva in a flesh-colored leotard, riding sidesaddle, her hair as long as her horse's tail. And, complete in red tunic, billowing pants and furry pillbox hat – a nasty Cossack!

But none of them could compete with Rodney. Nose in the dirt, he heaved and sighed his way around the ring, having endured the thousand-mile trek through the blizzards of the Russian winter.

We won the trophy!

As we trudged to center ring to receive it, I kept my head slumped on my chest to avoid the harrumphing looks from the hardworking women ringside, never mind the Cossack mom's murderous glare.

Shortly after this event, my parents sold Rodney to a friend for one dollar. He went on to become one of the top show jumpers in the countryside! Rodney! Just goes to show, we all have a passion somewhere deep inside us.

My next and last horse was my beloved Tim. He was a stunning Anglo-Arab with a sweet nature and a rocking lullaby of a canter that could only have been bestowed by God. His owner sold him because he had a severe sway back that eliminated him as a prospect for many hunter events that required the horse to be stripped of its saddle and paraded in front of the judge.

Although I showed Tim in classes judged solely on performance, I still wanted to camouflage his sway; so I stacked several blankets under the saddle to build up his hollow - a horse version of the padded bra. At fifteen, I entered Tim in a local horse show. When the ringmaster called us to trot, I squeezed my knees and moved Tim into the gait. But just as we reached the curve of the ring, I heard the all too familiar cry.

"Hawoooh hah! Evie! Take *hold* of that horse!"

I wanted to vaporize. It was bad enough that he yelled instruction, but did he have to yell my name?

In spite of Mr. Chambers' ringside coaching, Tim and I won a few ribbons, mostly seconds and thirds. Later that night, when Mom told me Mr. C was on the phone, I figured he wanted to congratulate me. I was wrong.

"What the hell were you doing in that ring today!" he barked. "His nose was out, no flexion. You didn't push him on to the bit. You looked like Sleeping Beauty out there."

I was hurt and furious and went to bed that night hating Mr. Chambers.

The following spring and summer, I worked tirelessly on Tim, and by fall, when we returned to the same show, we were no longer horse and rider; we were a single entity. When canter was called, I had only to think the command to send him into his rocking gait. We placed first in every class.

This presented a problem I had not anticipated. At the end of the day, as I mounted Tim for the eight-mile ride back to the ranch, the announcement echoed over the fairgrounds.

"All first and second place winners are to be stripped of their saddles and brought into the ring for final judging for the grand championship."

I felt sick. There was no way I was going to subject Tim to this humiliation, so I turned him in the direction of the fairground gates, gave him a boot and we took off, jumping both sides of the racetrack fence in our getaway. We'd almost cleared the property when two cowboys galloped up full tilt on either side of us.

"Miss! Miss, stop!"

I pulled Tim up.

"The judge is holding the class. He won't continue until that big bay of yours is in the ring."

Speechless with mortification, I followed them back to the show ring and dismounted. One of the cowboys, in an effort to help, un-cinched Tim's girth strap and slid off the saddle. Along with it fell the three saddle pads.

He looked on in shock.

"Oh," was all he could say.

I led Tim into the ring. We stood at the end of the row of contestants as the judge worked his way down the line. I held the reins behind my back. Tim nibbled gently on my fingers, looking for a treat.

When the judge, an elderly man with a sun creased face, arrived to view the horse he had already picked as champion, he took off his hat and smiled at me. Then, he walked around to take a look at Tim from the side. I could hear people laughing ringside. Laughing at Tim? Laughing at the judge who had missed the deformity? I don't know. All I *did* know was that I hated those people.

I stared at the ground. The judge came back to me and said gently, "It's too bad he's so low in the back."

I was in tears for most of the ride home. At the halfway point, Dad drew his car up beside me and rolled down the window.

"Now Eve, stop it. You won five first ribbons. So what if you didn't get the championship."

Did he not get it? I couldn't care less about the stupid cup. What I couldn't bear were people laughing at Tim – at my beautiful and gentle giant of a horse.

When I got home, I brushed Tim down and turned him into the pasture. I didn't want to go back to the house. I didn't want to see any of the stupid adults who just didn't *get* anything and kept whispering to each other that my moodiness was because I was going through that *stage*. I wiped my eyes on my shirtsleeve then started reluctantly down the road. Mr. Chambers was walking towards me from the house. I took a deep breath and steeled myself for another lecture.

We met at the halfway point. Mr. C. had one hand behind his back. With the other, he took off his dirty old fedora and held it to his chest. He looked solemn.

His blue eyes seared into me as he said, "I have never seen you ride so beautifully. You and that horse were *one*."

Then, he drew his hand from behind his back and presented me with a bag of sugared jelly candies.

"First prize, my dear," he said, softly.

In 1964, that bag of jellies cost twenty-five cents. It is the most spectacular trophy I have ever received.

Six years later, my passion for horses had been taken over by a passion for acting. I had been hired to perform in a play in Calgary. It was about the Welsh poet, Dylan Thomas. I played Caitlin, Dylan's wife. My parents organized a theatre party of thirteen to come see it, and Mr. and Mrs. Chambers were part of the group. Mr. C. was in his late eighties by then and had started to slip in and out of dementia. That night, I made my entrance and, thankfully, as my nerves melted away, settled into the scene with the actor playing Dylan.

It was then that I heard the bellowing cry.

"Haawoooh hah! There's Evie!"

The actor stared at me dumbfounded.

Members of the audience hissed, "Shhhh!"

Then I heard a shuffling sound that I found out later was one of the guests escorting Mr. C. out of the theatre. Somehow, the actor and I recovered and continued the performance.

The following Christmas, I went to visit Mr. C. It was the last time I would see him. He sat in the same armchair that my eight-year-old self had occupied years earlier when I devoured crumpets and tea. The fire crackled in the hearth, and as I sat cross-legged at Mr. Chambers' feet, he talked of foxhunting in the present tense, as if the two of us were riding home from the hunt, our horses' hooves echoing on the cobblestones of a Welsh village. Suddenly, he transitioned from his reverie to a moment of lucidity.

"You were so good in that play last summer, Evie."

"Thanks, Mr. Chambers," I answered, truly touched.

Then he said, "And you spoke such beautiful Welsh."

My eyes welled up as the memories flooded back with the tears. Of Mr. C's quiet voice counseling patience and gentleness. Of his harsher voice insisting on discipline and excellence. Of my yearning for his hard-won approval. No non-premiums there! I thought of tea, and crumpets, and of that wondrous bag of sugared jellies that sustained my spirit throughout my teen years.

And silently, I thanked him – for always noticing me.

Lucky Duck

My parents' marriage was not an episode from "Father Knows Best." The job, often referred to as "wife of," never sat well with Mom. It wasn't in her DNA to play second fiddle to anyone. However, with four young girls to care for and a husband whose legal career was on the ascendancy, she had no choice.

When I was ten, she disappeared down a dark hole of depression, where she stayed for a year. But when she wasn't laid flat by her depression, Mom found ingenious ways to express her "wife of" resentment.

What my father liked, better than anything else in life, was to hunt ducks. There is a paradox here. Dad was an avid conservationist, loved animals and worked with Ducks Unlimited to preserve the duck population.

"Is that so you can head south and shoot them in the fall?" I queried one afternoon, as I watched him pluck the feathers from a mallard.

"Eve, it's not shooting them as much as the experience of going with my friends to these old hotels, getting up before dawn, hiding with the dogs in the duck blind and watching the first light of dawn," he waxed lyrically.

23

Every fall he went off with his buddies, stayed in grungy hotels, shot ducks and came home, smelly but happy. He plucked and hung the birds, then pored over *The Joy of Cooking* in search of roast duck recipes. Sunday nights we gnawed through the tough meat, and as we spat out the gunshot, lied about how delicious it was.

Now when Dad came home happy, Mom, who had been left alone with us four girls, would make him pay. She resented his absence, but what she hated even more was that he could have such a good time without her. She didn't like his "Boy's Club." So, she set out to destroy it.

One day, she announced she had decided to take up hunting, that it sounded like a pile of fun, and that she wanted to join him on his trips. Not to worry, she would find someone to look after the kids.

Dad's face froze in feigned delight.

"Well that would be swell, Goofy (yes, he called her Goofy). But would you be comfortable? It's all men."

"But *you'll* be with me. It'll be nice to spend some time together."

"Well, that would be just... swell."

But first, she needed a gun. But it had to be a good one. She instructed Dad to go to Abercrombie and Fitch on his next trip to New York, pick out a gun, hip waders, boots, and a red hat with those ear flap thingies.

Then, she set about learning to shoot. For those of you not in the know, hunters practice shooting using clay discs. These fit into a trap which, when pulled, fling the discs into the sky. As a kid, I loved to pull the trap for Dad, to watch him track the disc across the sky, then blast it to pieces. He was a really good shot and probably got all but one during a session.

Once Mom had learned how to load and snap her gun shut, with much attention paid as to whether the "safety" switch was on or off, she and Dad headed out to the field. Over and over, Dad pulled the trap for her. Mom was not a good shot. If Dad missed one clay pigeon during practice, Mom only got one. But that did not deter her. Shooting ducks was not her mission. Wrecking the "Boy's Club" was. Or so she thought. But what she forgot about herself – and this is key – was that she was a born competitor. And that spelled trouble. With a capital T.

Their first official hunt took place on a cold November morning in a desolate place in southeast Alberta fittingly called Princess. How Dad explained Mom's presence to the "boys" I'll never know. Were they simply relieved they weren't married to Sheila, or did they fear this contagion might spread to their wives? Whatever the case, they all checked into a ramshackle hotel that was part of their "let's rough it" fun – "The Boys Camp Out." The two-story hotel had one washroom. The owner served a four AM breakfast in the small dining room, so the hunters could get out early to hide in their duck blinds.

The morning started out badly. Dad woke up. No Mom. He figured she was eating breakfast. Good. It was important to keep her fed. Unfed, she was a medical emergency, not just to herself but to anyone who crossed her path. Unfed, she was edgy, snarly and mean. She knew this about herself and always made sure she had sugar fixes at the ready. In her purse, pockets, or the glove compartment of her car, she kept stashes of lifesavers often mixed in with half melted Burnt Almond chocolate bars.

25

Eve Crawford

Dad, relieved Mom was getting fed, paddled down the hall in his long johns to the bathroom where, to his surprise, stood a long line of other hunters. Aside from dealing with bursting bladders, the men were frantic they might miss the magic hour when the ducks woke up or, even worse, that other hunters might beat them to their spot by the pond.

The first in line thumped on the door.

Silence.

He rattled the doorknob.

Silence.

"Anyone in there?"

At last, they heard the toilet flush followed by the sound of a running tap. Then the door opened and Mom strolled out, a McLean's magazine tucked under her arm. She glided regally past the men who, in unison, glared murderously at Dad.

An hour later, the men, plus Mom, were huddled in various blinds around the duck pond.

Picture this.

Duck decoys are bobbing up and down on the water. Mom and Dad lie side by side, Dad's trusty Labrador, Spike, at their side. Dawn is breaking. One of the men blows into his duck call. It emits a short, staccato quack. Moments later, the hunters hear a crescendo of quacking and beating wings as a flock of ducks begin to descend on the pond. The men rise from their blinds, load their guns, snap them shut, click off the safety switches, track the birds through the sky and, in turn, take their shots.

Dad hits one.

Mom stumbles to her feet, fumbles in her pocket, locates a bullet, loads, shoots – and misses.

This pattern continues throughout the day. Dad finally reaches his quota – there are government rules about these things – and his trusty lab, Spike, has retrieved them all. Mom is getting testy, and Dad knows it is crucial she get a duck. One of her very own. No pretending. No *"Sheila I am sure it was you who hit that one."*

She wasn't stupid.

The men conspire. They send her off with Spike to the other side of the pond and agree that none of them will shoot when the next birds fly by. If she simply points in the general direction of the flock, she's certain to bag something. Everyone settles. They can see the top of her red hat in the reeds across the water. All is quiet. The men, guns broken open, take swigs of scotch from their hip flasks, their day at an end.

Will George save his marriage? Will Sheila get a bird? Will she declare triumph and end her career so they can all get back to happier times – Boys Unlimited? Please God! Send ducks!

Their prayers are answered.

Distant honking, growing louder now, louder, an approaching cloud in the sky. Not a chance she could miss. The men peer through the reeds. They see Sheila stand, reach into her pocket for a bullet, load the gun, snap it shut, jam it into her shoulder and track the birds across the sky. They are overhead now.

"Shoot! Shoot!" hisses the all-male chorus. She points at the flock, but she doesn't fire! The ducks wing their way, unscathed, over the horizon.

Silence.

And then – Vesuvius.

"Bloody hell!"

Her red hat sinks out of sight in the distant reeds.

"I could murder you!"

That would be Dad, not the duck.

"Bloody, bloody hell!"

Dad, in his waders, squelches across the pond to find Mom sitting on a rock. Spike is at her side trembling – as he always did when there was an upset.

"What happened?" asks Dad.

"I don't know! It's this cheap gun you bought me! It doesn't work."

"It worked earlier today."

"Well it jammed. It wouldn't fire. It's a cheap gun. You bought me a cheap gun!"

"I got it at Abercrombie and Fitch!"

"Oh, so you say!"

"Did you take the safety off?"

"Don't be so condescending. Of course I did."

"Let me take a look."

Dad takes the gun. Sure enough, the safety is off.

"Did you load it?"

"Don't patronize me," she blubbers.

He cracks open the gun. Spies shiny silver where the brass end of the cylindrical shell should be. He tips the gun to empty the item into his hand. And out slides an unopened package of Butter Rum LifeSavers. Mom had thrown her collection of sweets into the same pocket as her shotgun shells.

Dad holds it up for her to see.

"Goofy," he chides.

"Oh," she says.

Reflexively, she looks over her shoulder to see if there is

anyone she can blame. No luck. The only option is to deflect. She takes Spike's head in her hands and squishes his face until folds of skin all but cover his worried brown eyes.

Putting her nose to his, she says, "Well Spike, that was one lucky duck."

Dad can contain himself no longer. He sinks down on the rock next to Mom, puts his arm around her and starts to laugh. Mom leans her head on his shoulder and joins in.

Spike stops shaking and licks Mom's face.

In the distance can be heard a single, contented quack.

The Family Class

The biggest show for the horsey set in 1950s Calgary was held in July at the Stampede Corral. Every year, competitors set up camp in large barns that had stalls for their horses plus an extra one that served as a tack room for riding equipment and feed. It was a huge social event. Parents joined each other for cocktail hour, sitting on picnic coolers in the hallway of the barn and pouring drinks from silver flasks. We kids mucked out the stalls, groomed our horses, and braided their manes and tails to get them show ready. Every night, we rubbed the horses' legs with liniment then bandaged them to prevent the swelling that would occur from standing overnight in their stalls. To this day, the smell of Absorbine makes me smile. They were happy times.

Until the Family Class.

A quick explanation. The class was a competition open to families riding under English or Western saddle. The drill was much the same as the RCMP's musical ride. Horses were ideally the same colour. Families were to ride abreast with the father on the outside next to the mother, then, in sequence, down to the youngest child. They were to walk, trot, canter, then reverse, in which case the family had to pinwheel around the father, with the horses on the outside moving faster to complete a seamless turn, leaving the youngest kid in full view.

The Family Class required cooperation and coordination, not

31

to mention a lot of practice. Our family never practiced. That would require a certain familial harmony – a quality we lacked, hence the naming of our ranch, Bedlam Ridge.

A friend of mine spent the summer with us when she was fifteen. She recalls returning from the barn to find my dad slumped in despair on the back porch of our cabin. A shrieking girl brawl could be heard from within.

He looked at her and said, "There is something seriously wrong with my genes, Brigid."

Brigid looked at Dad's pants, shook her head, and said, "I think your jeans look fine Mr. Crawford."

But back to the Family Class. Dad borrowed three chestnut horses from the Shriners who, in white shirts and red fezzes, performed their musical ride at the horse show. These horses matched the three chestnuts we had in our stable. The Shriner horses provided a distinct advantage, because they were all buddies and used to sticking together.

The evening of the class, Dad hurried to the stables from work. He presented all of us with white carnation boutonnières to pin in the lapel of our riding jackets. We were good to go; horses saddled up, boots polished. As we helped each other fasten our carnations, my father hurried into the tack room where he stripped down to his boxer shorts to don the riding habit Mom had brought from home: jodhpurs, crisp white shirt, stock tie and pin, and black riding jacket.

Dad had been a lieutenant in the navy and, used to being obeyed, barked orders at us five females as he unpacked his riding habit from the tote bag.

"Now look everybody," he said pulling out his jodhpurs, "you are to take the lead from *me* and *none* of you are to talk!"

Then he looked at the five of us, who were staring at what he was holding in his hand. His jodhpurs weren't jodhpurs. They were his ratty old long johns. The ones he wore every fall under his quilted hunting pants. He pawed through the tote bag. Nothing.

"Oh dear," said Mom, pressing her lips together.

"Damnit Sheila," he growled.

"Mom," I whined accusingly.

I always took Dad's side in their squabbles until, years later, I married and found out what having a husband was like.

But the family class was to begin in ten minutes. No time for finger pointing. Dad put on the long johns followed by his black riding boots. We all tried to convince ourselves that, between the top of his boots and the bottom of his jacket, never mind the odd gaping hole, you could hardly tell he was in his underwear. Mom announced that she would ride on the outside to keep him hidden. She told us we were to stick to Dad like glue so neither judge nor audience could see his "pants" for what they were.

Dad swung up into the saddle and, assuming a dignified posture, announced loudly, "But I'm still in charge!"

Mom stifled a laugh.

It started off well. The announcer, a well-known Calgary sports broadcaster, introduced each family as it entered the ring. The people in the stands oohed and ahhed at the beautifully turned out families with their cute little kiddies. This was the fifties, and everyone in Calgary knew everyone else.

Our name was called. We entered in parallel formation – the Crawford family: George and Sheila, or rather, *Sheila and George* with their four very cute daughters, all on matching chestnut horses. Mom was on the outside to hide Dad, then, in order of age, Sharon, Suzie, me, and Marti on her pony. Behind us was a family on pintos, resplendent in turquoise western gear, followed by a grouping of palominos.

To be clear, we were not in this for *fun*. We might have pretended

33

otherwise, but we *wanted* that trophy. The competition was stiff, but what we lacked in rehearsal and, let's face it, wardrobe – we made up in numbers.

Except for our archenemies, the Mortons. They rode just ahead of us – Mr. and Mrs. Morton with *their* four very cute daughters on matching black horses. They had beaten us the year before, but tonight it was game on! We had but three challenges.

1. The Morton family had practiced

2. Mr. Morton was wearing his jodhpurs, and –

3. Mr. Morton wasn't married to my mother. Dad was. And that, as it did so often, presented a problem.

The ringmaster was Major Atkinson, an elderly man dressed in brown, WWI riding gear. He called out orders on behalf of the judge, who stood next to him in the center of the ring. Using his hand-held megaphone, he called us to trot. When he issued the command, it always came out as two syllables, "TRO…OT!!!"

We did.

My horse, Rosie, didn't like Suzie's horse. She didn't know Suzie's horse. Suzie's horse was a well-trained Shriner's horse. So, Rosie, ears back, started to nip at the upstart. I gave her a quick boot and reined her in, hoping the judge had missed it, sandwiched as I was in the middle of the group.

"WA…ALK!"

We did. So far so good.

And then, "CAN…TER!"

Here, the trouble started. Dad, in his command voice, said, "Ok! On count of three."

But Mom didn't like his command voice. The war was over.

Dad started the count. "One… two… th– "

It was then that Mom booted her horse and took off, leaving Dad fully exposed in his long johns. He didn't wear the pants in the family! Not tonight anyway. Tonight, *she* was on the lead horse. But Mom was on a Shriner horse, as were Sharon and Suzie. And the Shriner horses were programmed to stick together, so they bolted forward to keep pace. Well, there was no way Marti and I were going to be left in the company of our pants-less father, so we booted our horses to catch up. There we were, the women in the family, deserting the lone male.

The announcer's voice boomed over the sound system, "Now Sheila, wait for George!"

Too late.

At this point, the Crawford women were a Molotov cocktail of chestnuts hurtling into the epicenter of the Morton family. Chaos. Chestnuts and blacks milling and kicking. Other families disbanding in panic to avert disaster. Pintos bucking, palominos rearing, kids falling off.

Major Atkinson alternately blew his whistle and yelled through his megaphone, "Walk, walk, WALK!" Then – "Halt, halt, HALT!"

But the only one at a halt was Dad, a statue in the middle of the ring. A man in his underwear with no place to hide.

Family class at the horse show.

A Song and a Dance

One Boxing Day, my mother stuffed herself into my hot pink leotard and danced the "Dying Swan" in our living room.

For guests.

It had been a rough Christmas. Marti and I were home from university, and the two of us, along with Mom and Dad, had come down with bronchitis. We had spent the week housebound, grumpy and sick – especially of each other.

Not only had we missed all the Christmas parties, but we couldn't even go to the Christmas dinner we traditionally celebrated with close friends at a neighbouring ranch. Mom was particularly bummed out, because she was missing the after-dinner caroling. She might not have been a good singer, but she was an enthusiastic one. Certain that everyone would miss her voice at the piano, she decided to record a solo then send the tape to be played at the after-dinner singsong.

Her choice?

"Somewhere My Love" from "Dr. Zhivago."

Ok, it wasn't a carol, but it did involve lots of sleighs and winter scenes.

Christmas afternoon, I was enlisted to set up the tape machine given to me that morning and flip the sheet music for her, while she pressed the echo pedal on our out of tune piano and, in between her wheezing and coughing, sang.

Mom had trouble hitting the high notes, so she was a bit afraid of them.

So were we.

She knew she faced a real challenge on the "whenever the spring breaks through" part of the song, so she started low. In a rattling growl that could scare the birds out of trees, she began.

Somewhere my love, there will be songs to sing,
Although the snow, covers the hope of spring.

She stopped momentarily, overcome by a spasm of coughing. "Oh dear," she croaked, as she reached for the toilet paper resting on the piano and blew her nose into a clump of it. Undaunted, she continued.

Somewhere a hill blossoms in green and gold.
And there are dreams,
All that your heart can hold.

Cough, wheeze, cough.

Someday, we'll meet again my love.
Someday – whenever the spring breaks –

Her fingers hovered over the keys. Everest confronted her. But it was game on.

In a low, wavering vibrato, she revved – a pole-vaulter hopping up and down. Then, she drew breath and went for it, swooping up, up, and over.

oooooooooooooooooo

oooooo   *oooooo*

Throoooo   *oooooooooooo!!!!!*

From the kitchen, Dad yelled, "That's enough Eve. Shut her down!"

Boxing Day, we were still feeling pretty moldy. Mom and Dad had planned to throw a party that night for thirty people. Certain that everyone would be tired of turkey, they decided to have the event catered and serve stew instead. But all that had been cancelled.

We managed to avoid each other for most of the day. Still in our shabby nightwear, we wandered in and out of rooms like inmates in an asylum. Around five o'clock, as the last trace of winter sun dipped behind the mountains, Dad passed through the living room, where I was snoozing, and into the kitchen to make a cup of tea.

Suddenly, I heard him yell.

"The stew, the stew!"

I leapt up and ran into the kitchen. Dad was looking out the front window. Coming down the road, was a white van.

"I forgot to cancel the stew!"

"Are you sure?"

"What else could it be?"

He turned.

"*You* answer the door Eve," he said, giving me a shove in the direction of the living room. He trailed behind me halfway then opened the door to the mini bar and hid behind it, which was pretty ridiculous considering the door stopped a foot above the ground and his ankles and worn leather slippers were in full view of the front entranceway.

The van pulled to a stop in the driveway.

I panicked.

"What'll I say?" I croaked, looking over my shoulder.

39

Dad's leather slippers did an agitated dance.

"Tell them – we don't live here."

A handsome, thirty-something man in a blue uniform, emerged from the van. In the name of propriety, I did up the top button of my flannel nightgown, then opened the door.

"Is this the Crawford residence?" he demanded.

"Yes, but we don't live here," I said, firmly.

He stepped past me into the house, stood at attention, and then unfurled a large scroll.

"Oyez, oyez, oyez –

I call upon you to yield up one George Lyndon Crawford Q.C.

Who has deliberately and unlawfully caused a legal contract to be rent asunder by virtue of a Breach of Promise of Marriage to wit the solemn betrothal of his daughter Sharon Jane Crawford to one David Gordon Milner, the son of the Plaintiff, Donald Milner, entered into in the year 1941.

We hereby claim damages in the amount of one million dollars or, in lieu of that, the several bottles of Chivas Regal that George Crawford keeps hidden from guests in his dog box."

"Oh for God's sake," said Dad, stepping out from behind the bar door. At the same time, five people crawled out of the back of the van bearing bottles of booze, food and laughter. It was the Milner family, led by their patriarch, Donnie, whose drinking glass hung from his neck on a chain.

Donald Milner, a Justice of the Supreme Court of Canada, and his wife, Daisy, had been close friends of my parents at university in the thirties. In fact, they had been responsible for Mom and Dad getting back together after a tough break-up. During a drunken celebration after Daisy had won the Exacta at the Calgary horse races, Donnie noted that Dad looked pretty gloomy.

"Where's that Sheila Stewart?" he asked.

"Vancouver," sighed Dad, "but she wants nothing to do with me."

So Donnie quickly composed a singing telegram and had it sent to my Mom – from Dad. The message, and I am not sure Dad was aware of this, was a proposal of marriage which the pimply, teenaged messenger sang in his breaking voice to Mom. She accepted.

The rest is history – well not quite.

Two years later, Daisy gave birth to their son, David. The next day, Mom gave birth to Sharon. The two fathers decided to draw up a contract of marriage, committing these babes to one another. And it was this breach of contract that the now thirty-year-old David had read in our entranceway.

The Milners flooded into our house, and, before we knew it, other close friends were invited over. A party! Every doctor's prescription for cabin fever.

Which brings me to the Dying Swan.

As the evening progressed, my mother, whose thwarted singing endeavor of Christmas Day still weighed on her, decided to cut her losses and change careers. Taking me to one side, she announced solemnly that she would dance. But it wasn't to be just *any* dance. She would perform the solo from Tchaikovsky's Swan Lake. She would dance the *Dance of the Dying Swan*.

But she needed my help.

We retreated to my bedroom. I grabbed the hot pink leotard I wore to dance class. Who said the swan had to be white?

As Mom struggled into it, she gasped, "What about feathers?"

41

I located a bright green quill pen that had been given to me years earlier and stuck it into her hair. She grabbed my silk dressing gown and tied it around her ample waist as a sash.

"You're to introduce me by my maiden name, Sheila Stewart," she instructed.

As she waited "backstage" around the corner from the living room where the festivities were escalating, I slid over to the record player that sat in a cabinet at the side of the room. Rifling through our record collection, I found lots of Broadway albums but it was pretty sparse pickings in the classical music department. Not a "Dying Swan" to be found. All I could find was the Nutcracker Suite. I reported this to Mom who was doing a warm up plié in the hallway.

"That's ok. It's still Tchaikovsky," she said, waving me off with a graceful sweep of her arm.

I hushed the crowd, introduced her, and with that, my mother, channeling her inner Pavlova, pushed up onto her toes and fluttered into the living room to the twinkling, playful music of the Sugar Plum Fairy. Cheers and whistles ensued.

But an unforeseen problem presented itself. It's not *easy* to die to the "Sugar Plum Fairy."

Try it.

Also, as much as the high notes had defeated her the day before, falling to the ground, a necessary element for any death scene, proved challenging. In her mid-sixties, she was not as flexible as memory served. But she soldiered on. Twirling round and round, she flapped her "wings" and, every once in a while, threw in a real crowd pleaser – a gravity defying *jeté*.

As she started to tire, I saw her cast a worried look downwards. If the high note from Zhivago was Everest, the living room floor was "Twenty Thousand Leagues Under the Sea."

42

"Die, die, die!" yelled the crowd.

"I'm trying, I'm trying," she wheezed to her fans.

Dad grabbed my microphone.

"Poor Sheila, she wants to die, but she just can't get down."

Mom started to laugh, which in turn set off wracking coughs that caused her to collapse on a nearby chair to the cheers and bravos of her fans.

Donnie took a sip from the glass still hanging from his neck. Then, he rose to speak. A hush fell over the audience.

In the solemn voice that for years had issued verdicts from the highest court in the land, he made this pronouncement.

"Some have seen Nureyev. Some have seen Fontaine. But until you have seen Sheila Stewart *die*, you haven't *lived*."

When Mom died at ninety-four, we buried her next to Dad in a country cemetery that overlooks the Rocky Mountains. Engraved on her stone is a pair of ballet slippers on point and, courtesy of Lord Byron, this inscription.

On with the dance,
Let joy be unconfined!

PART II

Dear Peggy

Tim and me

New best friends

Mrs. Chambers

My first professional role

Dracula

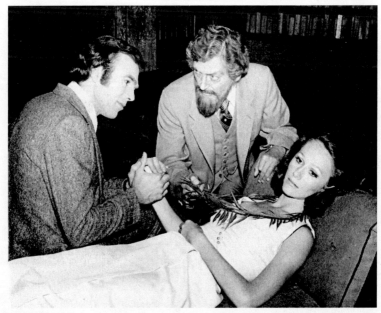

To: Margaret McNab
*Re: **The last 30 years***

Dear Peggy,

I can't believe they reported me as deceased at the school reunion! That is so rude! Just because I never replied to those stupid alumni donation requests. Anyway, thanks for tracking me down. As I write this, I realize you're the only one who seems to have cared. How did I die? Did anyone say? I'll bet this was the work of that bitch, Moira Whittaker. She's wanted me dead ever since I clobbered her in the girls' badminton finals. Remember that?

We were in the third game, tied at ten each. She'd just won serve after a five-minute rally. I was doubled over with a stitch, completely on the ropes. Then, I caught the smug look on her pert, self-satisfied little face.

"Are you ok, Eve?"

That did it!

She served high to the back line. I faked an overhead return, pulled a last-minute switch, then dropped it into the opposite corner for the point. Ha! My serve. I whipped it high to the back, she hit a weak return to mid-court, and then I leapt up and smashed it down her throat for the championship!

Moira Whittaker. God she was competitive.

Speaking of badminton, do you still have your trophy? I do. I'm drinking out of it right now – in celebration of our *détente*.

Well, well, well. It took my reported demise for you to lay down your arms. That, plus you finally realizing I was right about that wiener of a guy you married. Ok, I never should have opened my big, fat mouth. Sorry. I'm just pissed off that it cost us thirty years of friendship. But then, you always *were* stubborn Peggy.

Luckily, *I'm* patient.

If it's any solace to you, I married a weenie of my own. How was your divorce? Mine took three years and cost $100,000. Other than that, it was fine.

Seriously partner, it is good to hear from you, because, let's face it, we were a magic combination. The Mutt and Jeff of the courts. "Girls' Doubles Champs – *Guthrie School for Young Ladies.*"

Ha! Well, they tried!

Speaking of *young* ladies, you say you knew I was still alive when you saw me in that soup commercial playing, and I quote, "a tired old crone." That was not me you douche bag! It was my ugly older sister. God, I hate this business. Actors have to age publicly and in close-up!

Pegs, I hooted when you said I must be doing well in my career. To tell you the truth, I've never really felt I *had* a career. I keep meaning to have one. I write mission statements that say I'm *going* to have one. But life keeps getting in the way.

I quit the stage just before my first son, Luke, was born. Gads. That's eighteen years now. I couldn't stay awake long enough to perform, never mind get up in the morning to look after –

No. That's not true. That's not why I quit. I've never told this to anyone Peggy, but hey, I've never lied to you, so why start now?

I quit… because of a bad review.

Oh brother.

I'd had good and bad over the years, but there was one in particular that did me in. I was in a production of Sean O'Casey's "The Plough and the Stars." It's set during the 1916 Easter uprisings in Dublin. I played pregnant Nora who begs her husband not to go to war. He goes anyway. She has a miscarriage at the end of the third act. By the fourth act, when she finds out her husband's been killed, she goes mad from grief. In those days, people didn't get "depressed." They went mad. Way more exciting.

I hadn't had kids at that point, so I did all sorts of research about the nature of labour pains in order to be specific and accurate during the miscarriage scene. But this wasn't just about a miscarriage. It was about a woman's loss. Loss of her child, her husband, her sanity. As an actor, I decided I wasn't going to play it safe. So, I went for it.

Picture this.

It's opening night, end of the third act. The lights are on a slow fade to black as I, Nora, fall to my knees, clutch my belly and emit a carefully modulated crescendo of screams that I had worked on for three weeks, at sixty bucks an hour, with my voice coach. The audience went silent; you could have heard a pin drop.

After the show, the cast members told me the effect was bone chilling. The director said he was proud of me for taking such risks.

The next morning, I ran to the newspaper box and flipped

through the paper looking for the review that my parents and all their friends would read in Calgary. Found it, skimmed through looking for my name – actors don't care about anyone's notice but their own – and there it was.

"Eve Crawford's onstage miscarriage was reminiscent of a yak in labour."

A yak! I didn't even know what a yak was! I ran home, grabbed the dictionary and there, alongside the definition, was a picture.

Peggy! Have you ever seen a yak? It's an ugly, hairy ox that lives in Tibet. Ok, I hear you laughing. I'm laughing as I write this – sort of. But then? I wasn't playing it for laughs *then*, Peggy. All I felt was utter embarrassment that my hard worked-on performance had drawn such public derision.

Now this particular critic was known for coming to the theatre with his *"babe de jour"* and making out through many of the performances. Maybe my onstage screams had soured the mood. Anyway, he wasn't entirely respected in theatrical circles. But the public at large didn't know that. The public at large, including my parents' friends, regarded this newspaper as the truth made word. And they all phoned to comment and to laugh. Except my mom. She phoned to ask if I was all right.

"I'm fine Mom. It's just a stupid review."

But I wasn't fooling her.

There were twenty-eight performances left to go after that. Every night, as I stood in the wings waiting to go on, all I wanted was a large bag to put over my head. And oh, how I dreaded getting to that scene – the scene that was key to my performance. All I could think of was this ugly, hairy beast moaning in the snow-covered Himalayas, and I felt fear. I tightened up and backed away from my commitment to the scene. I lost my bravery. And once you lose that, you've got to step down.

As luck would have it, I got pregnant for real soon after the show closed, and the birth of my son was the perfect excuse never to return to the stage.

It's odd, Peggy. When I was little, I acted to get attention, to get approval. *Look at me, look at me!* And people did, because I was a kid. But here's the paradox. If you love acting and decide to go into it for real, you enter a profession that is the most brutal of them all for approval seekers.

After quitting the stage, I stuck to the safer world of film where, as long as I played small parts, nobody would notice me. I'm the "Where's Waldo" of Canadian film.

That sassy, attention-seeking little show-off grew up to discover that true happiness lay in not getting noticed at all.

Ain't that just the Canadian experience!

Until last year. Last year, I did a nice, fat part in a film with Julie Andrews. Got lots of positive reaction. The New York Times declared *me*, Eve Crawford, a "find." Disney and ABC execs asked the director, "Where did you *find* her?"

I was on cloud nine. At the age of fifty-two, I had been discovered. And after the show was aired, and the reviews came out, and people phoned to congratulate me, you'll never guess what happened!

Nothing.

I didn't work again for six months. And when I finally *did* get a job, it was to play a sad but "understanding" wife in a training film on erectile dysfunction for a bunch of doctors in San Diego.

From Julie Andrews to Erectile Dysfunction – a day in the life of a Canadian actor.

I was back to square one, convincing people I was good enough to say a line. But the worst of it was that the people I had to convince were just slightly older than my skateboarding son, Luke.

A few years ago, I was hired to play a small part in a film with Warren Beatty. But that wasn't the best part. The best part was I got to go to L.A. to do it. My marriage, at this point, was on its last legs. I was exhausted, confused and scared. I needed to get away.

So, there I was, the morning of my departure, cramming the last items into my suitcase. I was sweaty and stressed as I screamed final instructions to my husband and kids.

"The fish has been pooping pink playdough for three days! You better take him to the vet. There are four 'good to go' dinners in the freezer. And there's some green fungus thingy growing on the bottom of Luke's foot. Health cards are in your golf bag with your balls."

Then, Peggy, I saw it. The limo the film company had sent to pick me up. Out gets the driver, this elegant, elderly man dressed in black tie. He even had a carnation pinned to his lapel! He opened the passenger door, then stood to the side at attention – the way the secret service guys do for the President.

The universe had finally figured out that this was the way Eve Crawford was meant to live! I swanned out of the house, slid into the backseat of the limo, waved a sad goodbye to my boys, whose sticky little faces were plastered to the front window, then flew to Hollywood – *first class!* – where I happily became part of the reflecting pool for Warren Beatty.

I worked, I slept, I ordered up room service, I watched TV. I had full control of the flicker! I shopped, I walked on the beach, I did yoga, I got rested, and then – I came back home and asked for a divorce. But that's another story.

My point is this. When I got back, alive with the sense of having been appreciated and respected and treated like a queen, my agent sent me to a commercial audition. The product was dishwasher detergent.

Now, when you audition for a commercial, the drill is this: You walk into a room where a group of people, usually wearing black, sit behind a long trestle table laden with croissants and fruit that some of the less respectful will munch on while you audition. That's if they're not on their cell phones.

Like a well-trained dog, you stand on an X marked on the floor, look into the camera then slate your name and agency.

"Hi, I'm Eve Crawford with the Noble Caplan agency."

Then, you turn sideways to show them your profile.

This day, the director, who was all of twenty years old, says, "Yo, Eve, tell us quickly, what's been goin' down with you lately?"

"Well… I've just come back from LA where I was working on a film with Warren Beatty!"

"Who?"

Then, all business, he says, "Now, the set-up is this. You are throwing a humongous dinner party, and you're pretty wigged out. You've run out of plates and go to grab a clean one from the dishwasher. But there's this leftover shit stuck to the plate. Just as you start to chip it off with your finger, this fat ass poser chick comes in and catches you. You shoulda' had a spotter. You are completely humiliated. End of scene."

"Ok," I chirp, "do you have a plate I can work with?"

"No need. We just want to be sure you can do a real embarrassed expression. So, how 'bout looking into camera and

55

telling us about – the most humiliating sexual experience of your life."

Peggy! I was 48 years old! I was the mother of two children and had been a professional actor for twenty-six years. And this little twerp – I swear he'd been at one of Luke's sleepovers – wanted me to talk about the most humiliating sexual experience of my life? Remember the divorce? I couldn't remember when I'd last had sex! Plus, I knew, I just *knew*, that these guys were going to save the tape and play it at their agency's Christmas party. But, I really wanted this job and was determined to prove that after twenty-six years of doing Chekov, Shakespeare and Shaw, that, yes! I had the talent to muster an expression of embarrassment over a dirty dish, and that I could do it better than any of the other fifteen actors they had called in for the part.

So, I looked at the director and said, "Well, I'm not going to tell you about the most humiliating sexual experience of my life, but I *will* tell you about my very embarrassing visit to parliament – that's in Ottawa by the way – on a winter's day in 1973."

I looked into the camera and continued.

"I was at the entrance to the visitor's gallery, when an ancient security guard blocked my passage to check my purse for bombs.

"'You're in luck Miss. There's one seat left in the middle of the row.'

"Then, in a quavering voice, he confided, 'Should be an exciting afternoon. They're debating the *Notwithstanding Clause!*

"The visitor's gallery is very steep and a total hazard to anyone with vertigo. Also, there is very little room to pass in front of people without falling into the row below. Everyone in the gallery was male and wearing a headset. Since English was being spoken on the floor of the house, this meant that these guys were all French. *Merveilleux*! I carefully squeezed by the men.

"Pardon. Excusez-moi. Merci.

"I was one seat away from my destination when this really hot guy looked me right in the eye, then slowly pulled back the cord of his headset to ease my passage. I could feel the electricity surge between us. Well, the excitement must have been too much, because, just as I edged past him, my foot slipped off the ledge hurtling me into my seat and – I stuck my finger up his nose!

"What did I do?

"I extracted it.

"Then, I looked down at the House of Commons and thought and thought. What now? Nothing, *nothing* in life had prepared me for this.

"At 'The Guthrie School for Young Ladies,' we had to take charm lessons – to make us suitable for marriage. We learned to sit sideways, cross legs at the ankles sideways, walk down the stairs sideways. We did everything sideways, so no boys could ever look up our skirts. But were we ever told what to do if, by chance, we stuck a finger up a Frenchman's nose? *Nooo!*

"I could sense the guy reeling from the shock. I snuck a sideways peek to see if he had a nosebleed. Phew! Nothing so far.

"Since a date was now out of the question – can you imagine the speeches at the wedding! – I decided the only decent thing to do was to pretend it didn't happen. But that wasn't easy, because my finger was wet, and I wasn't a mother yet, so I wasn't used to gross things. All I could do was sit there and let my digit dry in the hot air blowing up from the "notwithstanding" debate below. When I thought a decent amount of time had gone by, I summoned up every ounce of charm instilled in me at the 'Guthrie School for Young Ladies,' and exited. Sideways of course.

"And that was my visit to parliament in 1973."

Well, Peggy, the room was silent. The black bedecked suits just stared at me. Their cheeks were bulging with half chewed croissants. But the director? He loved it!

"Whoa, momma! You actually stuck your finger up that philosopher's nose? That is so butter. That is beach sex."

"Do I get the part?" I asked.

"No. You have red hair and you're too old. But thanks for coming in."

And do you know what I said, Peggy?

I said, "Oh, you're welcome."

And in that one audition, the entire Hollywood experience was knocked right out of me. Once again, I was a forelock-tugging Canadian actor.

Oh, thank god! I hear skateboards on the approach. That'll be my sixteen-year-old Luke and his friend, "Shitface." Shitface is white, has dreadlocks and a chipped front tooth. His mother calls him Eric. He's coming for a sleepover.

Ok Peggy, your turn. Write back, and tell me about *your* life as a nurse. Now that *is* a career!

Tons of love and – at long last – thirty years of Great, Big Hugs!

Eve

To: Margaret McNab
*Re: **Barometer Falling***

Peggy,

Good Lord, you sound like my mother. I never should have told you why I quit the theatre! Yes, I promise! Before I die, I'll hunt down that bratty little show-off I used to be. I know I've turned into the cowardly lion! I've had a team of therapists working on my self-esteem for the past ten years. They just haven't come up with the answer yet. But fear not; I'm on the case. Because more than anything else, I want the inscription on my tombstone to read:

"Here lies the girl who clobbered Moira Whittaker"

But enough about my life. You run the sexually transmitted disease clinic for all of Vancouver. And you think *my* life is dramatic? You deal with drama on a daily basis! You save lives!

I was thinking about you and me and the paths we've taken, and I thought of this Chinese saying:

"If I had but two yen, I would spend one on food, that I might live, and the other on a flower, to make life worth living."

Maybe that's what the two of us are about. You help people live, and, from time to time, I help them laugh – or cry.

Survival and art.

Though, I must say, some productions I've been in were more about survival than art. I remember one in particular.

At twenty-three, I spent a few months doing summer stock in the Maritimes. The drill was this: We'd rehearse one play during the day, perform a different one at night, go to the bar after the show to get drunk, then back to wherever we were staying to learn lines for the following day. You had to be young.

The first play of the season was called "The Patrick Pearse Motel," and, as you might guess, was set in Ireland. It was what we call in the biz a "bedroom farce." Usually, there are beds on stage, be they in hotels or brothels, husbands looking for wives, wives looking for husbands, lots of mistaken identity with people running in and out of bedrooms in various forms of undress. All innocent fun and a great favourite with the summer crowd.

In this production, I played the vampy English motel manager, Miss Manning. I was decked out in mini skirt, boots, low cut top, lots of hair, false eyelashes etc.

One night, mid performance, I was playing a scene with one of the "cheating husbands." This character, Dermott, had had a previous fling with Manning and wanted to continue where they had left off. The lusty Dermott was played by Jack, a slightly built British actor who was a tad effeminate – or maybe just English. Midway through the play, the two of us were standing centre stage playing a scene where Dermott/Jack is trying to get me/Manning into bed again. I can't remember the exact lines, but they went something like this:

Jack/Dermott (in a really good Irish accent): Oh me darlin', what could be the harm in a slap and a tickle – just for old times' sake?

Me/Miss Manning (in a really bad English accent): The harm! Last time we were together, you used me up! Then you…

It was at this point that a man drifted onstage and into my peripheral vision. Who was he? He wasn't in our scene! But I was a professional, well-trained in focus and the whole "show must go on" bit, so I ploughed on with my lines.

Me/Manning: …you, you used me up! Then you tossed me aside like an old bed sock!

The man started to speak. It was Walter, artistic director of the theatre! He had his back to us and was talking to the audience.

"Ladies and gentlemen, the theatre has just received a phone call. If you come to the box office tomorrow, you will receive a full refund for tonight's performance. Now, I must ask you to exit the theatre as quickly and quietly as possible."

Peggy, this was the early seventies. The IRA had been carrying out numerous terrorist attacks in Britain – among them, bombings in London's West End theatre district. No better way to disrupt tourism than to phone in a bomb threat, right? The British actors had behaved splendidly under trying circumstances and, as captains of the ship, showed the patrons where the exits were, leaving only after the last audience member had been evacuated.

Now, I am sure that I would have done the same had it not been for the book I was reading that summer. In my effort to better understand the Maritimes, I had taken "Barometer Rising" out of the local library. It was a novel that centered on the Halifax explosion in World War One. In December of 1917, two ships collided in the city's harbor. One of them, a munitions ship, was loaded with explosives bound for the battlefields of Europe. The result was the largest man-made explosion prior to the detonation of the atomic bomb in 1945.

And get this! The explosion was so powerful that it hurled the ship's anchor more than two miles over the city, where it embedded itself in a hilltop.

So you see, aside from my lines, massive explosions were front of mind. If I hadn't been reading that book, I know I would have turned to the audience and, with a flight attendant's reassuring smile, made sweeping motions with my arms to indicate the fore and aft exits.

But all I could envision was the anchor. All I could see was me, Miss Manning, projected like a missile through the roof of the theatre, rocketing across the sky, to be found years later, embedded in that same hilltop; a single boot sticking out of the grassy slope.

So, I did what any sensible person would do under the circumstance.

I looked at Walter, then I looked at Jack, and then, in front of an audience of seven hundred people, I screamed, "IT'S A BOMB, IT'S A BOMB!"

Now, if there was a more cowardly lion than me, it was Jack. His eyes widened in panic. Then, as if on cue, the two of us slammed straight into each other in our effort to escape. But I was heftier than Jack, so I heaved him aside and ran. I think he landed on one of the motel beds. I didn't look back to find out. Let *him* be the anchor! Me? I ran screaming through the dark recesses of the backstage and out the exit to the parking lot where, heart pounding, I took refuge under a street lamp.

Police cars, sirens wailing, converged on the theatre. Then, from underneath my lamplight of shame, I watched as audience members strolled out in an orderly fashion. Mortified, I crept from under the light's glare and into the shadows. How could I have behaved in such a disgraceful manner? I had to recoup. And the only way to do that was to pretend – that I hadn't done what I had done.

So, I stepped back into the light and, in my best Air Canada voice, said, "Is everyone alright? It's probably just a prank. I'm sure there's no bomb. Unless, of course, they were referring to the show. Hahaha."

But people weren't buying it. Contempt would have been preferable to their sad dismissal of my sorry self.

Trailing after the last audience member came the crew, followed by the cast. And guess who was the last one out Peggy? Jack! Had he done the British thing and waited for everyone to evacuate? Make me look bad why don't you, Jack! Then, I saw he was limping. Phew!!!

In the pulsating lights of the bomb squad cars, I glimpsed the contemptuous looks from my cast mates. They obviously had not read "Barometer Rising."

Time to divert.

"Hey guys, what say we go over to the Lord Beaverbrook for a drink?"

Nothing is more tempting to an actor either before, during, or after a show than the promise of a little "cheerio" as a friend of mine used to call her cocktail. Don't get me wrong. We're not alcoholics. Not all of us. It's just that any relief from our customary operating state of high adrenaline is welcome. And this situation was high adrenaline.

I might have waved a wand. The group turned en masse and headed obediently across the road to the hotel. I followed, keeping a good distance between Jack and myself.

Peggy, you may remember from our university days that alcohol is not my friend. Wasn't it you who held my head over the toilet as I hurled the three Baby Ducks I'd knocked back from some guy's Quack Pack at that frat party? Thanks for that by the way. That experience seems to have sensitized me for life. Two drinks for me is a tear. Three – a trip to emergency.

But bomb night was an exception. I needed alcohol for two reasons. One, to calm my frazzled state. Two, to obliterate all memory of my shameful public display. So, I squeezed into a semi-circular booth with some of the cast and crew and ordered my first beer. And here is the best part. Next to me was this gorgeous guy, whose name I shall not mention because – I cannot remember it. He was the theatre's production manager; blonde ponytail, five o'clock shadow, tall, lean with intense blue eyes. I think he was Russian. Recently, he had had an argument that ended in a fistfight with this big hulk of a lighting man called Bud, so named for the tattoo of said beer on his arm. And my guy – I'll call him Guy – won! It was so primitive. He was a true "bad boy," and I'd had a crush on him all summer but had been too shy and tongue-tied to let him know.

But bomb night was a leveler. By beer six, I was leaning into him, laughing merrily, at which point he whispered into my ear to ask if I wanted to go back to the theatre with him to lock up. The Mounties had swept the building for explosives, and all was clear.

"Well, sure," slurred I, seductively.

Back across the road we staggered – well I did – and in the darkened theatre, we made the rounds to make sure all was sealed tight. In the dim glow of the ghost light hanging over the stage, we climbed up onto the set on our way to lock the back exit, the one I had fled through hours before. And lo and behold! There, before us, was the bed of one of the two "motel rooms."

Well! To quote that well-known Roman slave, Publilius Syrus, "Opportunity is often lost by deliberating."

And deliberation on Bomb Night was a nonstarter. Guy and I threw ourselves onto that bed and went at it. Or, started to. But combine the sudden change of altitude with a lot of rocking and rolling, and what do you get?

"Ohhhhhh. OHHHHHH!" My groans crescendoed in the darkened theatre as, with one boot on and one boot off, I staggered backstage to, repeatedly and loudly, hurl six beers into to the garbage can next to the stage manager's desk.

Ghastly, you say?

Well no!

What I didn't know was that my delicate constitution had saved me from an embarrassment way more humiliating than my earlier cowardice. The next day, an actress in our cast who had been playing "hide the salami" with Guy's archenemy, Bud, told me that he, too, had returned to the theatre that night to check on the security of the lighting booth. From his perch at the back of the theatre, Bud heard the two of us laughing and canoodling. He was waiting for our little scene to reach its – ahem – climax, before he pulled the lever to flood the stage with light. But my bilious stomach robbed him of his revenge.

The next night, Walter came backstage before the show to see how we were all doing.

"What exactly happened last night, Walter?" I asked.

"I was in my office working while you guys were on stage. The phone rings and some guy says, 'You know there's a bomb in there?'"

He reassured us that he had our backs, not to worry, and that he would see us after the show.

65

This is a terrible admission Peggy, but in my longing for redemption, I secretly hoped there would be another threat. I had spent the afternoon in my hotel room practicing evacuation lines in my Air Canada voice. But no such luck. The performance went without a hitch.

After the show, Walter came backstage.

"So, Walter, no phone call tonight?"

He looked at me and shrugged.

"I don't know. I took the phone off the hook."

Yikes Pegs! I just looked at the time. I have an audition in the morning for an English nun. I hate those accenty, no-make-up parts. Gotta get my beauty sleep so I can look like Audrey Hepburn.

Restrain yourself,
Reverend Mother Eve

To: Margaret McNab
Re: ***Blood lust***

So, Peggy, my little novice, how was my English nun audition, you ask? Do you know what the director said to me? He asked if I could be a little more motherly and a little less superior; that I didn't come over as a servant of God. Sheesh! I've been working on my fucking heart chakra all week!

You wanted to know if, after my public and very loud display of cowardice, I ever worked at that theatre again? Your use of the word cowardice is rather harsh. My reaction was an entirely reasonable flight response in the face of imminent danger. Not everyone in this world can do the "keep calm and carry on" thing. Someone has to get scared, or how can others shine?

But in answer to your question, no, I was never asked back. But it wasn't the bomb scare that did me in. The final nail in the coffin occurred during the second show that summer, when I suffered the tiniest lapse in professional behavior.

Speaking of coffins, the play was "Dracula." You know Dracula don't you Pegs – the Romanian count who is part of the "undead?" He sleeps in a coffin during the day, sucks blood out of virgins at night, and turns himself into a bat from time to time. He's your basic sick fuck.

In our production, this terrific actor, David Brown, played Dracula. He'd had a lot of dance training so carried himself in the courtly, elegant manner that the part demanded. Every night, he glued on this flattened plasticine nose and these black, lightning bolt eyebrows to make him look more bat-like. David was blonde, so he blackened his hair and greased it back in the style of the day, and since no one had a clue what a Romanian accent was like, he settled for a pretty good imitation of Zsa Zsa Gabor. Not bad for four days rehearsal.

I played the sweet, virginal Lucy who gets her neck bitten – a vampire form of deflowering – and then, in her anemic state, turns into an evil vamp with a blood lust of her own. The only way to save Lucy is to finish off Dracula.

The guy brought in to do all this was Professor Van Helsing, played by an accomplished, if somewhat overweight, actor, well – three hundred pounds – with a pretty bad case of asthma.

There was one kick-ass scene in the middle of the show, where Van Helsing is alone on stage, looking in the mirror and chatting to his reflection about how this vampire hunting has taken a toll on his looks. Meanwhile, backstage, David/Dracula climbs on a stool, grabs this trapeze, and swoops in through the window, releasing the bar just in time to make it look like he's flying. He lands quietly behind Van Helsing, who doesn't know he's there. Vampires' images can't be reflected, you see. Only when Dracula says, very Zsa Zsa-like, "Gud eeeevening prrrofesseur," does Van Helsing whirl around and say breathlessly, which was easy because of his wheeze, "Count, I did not hear you! Your footstep is so light."

Well, the audience loved it!

But one night, they loved it even more and for all the wrong reasons.

Picture this.

It's the middle of the show. The actors are doing their thing on stage. David and I are hanging around in the darkened wings, waiting for our entrance cues. We're fanning ourselves, because it is 100 degrees Fahrenheit outside, and there is no air conditioning in the theatre, and the two of us, particularly David, are getting pretty sticky. Remember, he's in a tuxedo, complete with scarlet lined cape, wearing black wool socks and patent leather shoes, plus the plasticine nose and glued-on eyebrows. Well, he was so sweaty that I decided to distract him from his misery by telling him the story of how my sister Marti tried to get out of a goodnight kiss.

Careful not to disturb the actors onstage, I whispered, "She stood in the doorway of her apartment, and right in front of her date, started in on this big bag of prunes!"

"Did she eat the whole thing?" asked David.

"Yes!"

"Did it work?"

"No! The guy was a pig farmer and was used to waiting for things – like spring. He waited 'til she finished the whole bag, then he kissed her!"

David was aghast.

"I've never wanted to kiss a girl that much."

So you see, Peggy, it worked! David forgot his discomfort.

Unfortunately, he forgot something else. His entrance! His big, bat flying through the window scene, entrance!

Suddenly, a stage hand is at his side, hissing, "David! You're on!"

I had made him miss his entrance!

Peggy, do you know what it is like when you miss an entrance?

Your heart stops. You enter a hollow, mindless state, during which you get transported in an adrenaline rush to where you should be, but you have no memory of how you got there. Once you're on stage, heart pounding at two hundred beats a minute, you face your shell-shocked fellow actor who has been left standing on stage in front of several hundred people with nothing to say!

In a nano-second, David leapt on the stool and reached for the bar of the trapeze. Van Helsing is onstage looking into the mirror, waiting to be startled. David lets fly. But, there was this little nail backstage, and his cape got caught on it, and just as he's about to let go of the trapeze to land "soundlessly" on the other side of the window sill, he gets whiplashed back through the window out of sight. All the audience sees of him is a glimmer of his shiny, patent shoes. Then, they hear a loud crash backstage, followed by a very un-Zsa Zsa-like, "Fuck!"

Bereft of his trapeze, David, in a fury, yanks his cape from the nail. Now what? No other option. He climbs through the window. So, the next thing the audience sees, is a single, patent leather shoe, followed by a second patent leather shoe with a very unkempt Dracula attached. His carefully greased hair is hanging in a large clump over his forehead revealing the, not so dark for the Count of Darkness, blonde underneath. But David is a pro. He sweeps his hair, very Zsa Zsa-like, back into place, straightens his cape, assumes second position from his dancing days, takes a breath, and is about to deliver his "Gud eeevening prrrrofessssseur" to Van Helsing's waiting back, when disaster strikes again.

Remember the heat wave? Add to that the stress of the last few moments, and you've got a lot of sweat. The glue gave out.

OK:

An eyebrow fell off. One lightning bolt eyebrow. And it's lying there in front of him like a big, squashed caterpillar. The hairy kind.

By this time, Van Helsing, still looking steadfastly in the mirror, has run out of things to say to himself and started to floss his teeth. Meanwhile, behind him, Dracula is missing his eyebrow. And he's not going to proceed without it. How could he? Who's going to take a vampire with one eyebrow seriously? So, he raises his tattered cape to cover his face from the audience, does a graceful plié, scoops up his brow, and sticks it back in place. Well, not quite in place. And that was the final straw, because, well, call me unprofessional, but it's really hard to act opposite a guy who has an eyebrow in the middle of his forehead.

This is what happened.

At the end of the second act, I/Lucy, in my anemic state, am alone on stage, sleeping on the settee. Enter Dracula. Bathed in a green light, he stands a few feet away then slowly raises his arms and spreads his cape. Cue the organ music! Trance-like, I arise and float over to him. He drapes me over his arm, raises his face to the audience, bares his fangs and then plunges them into my neck, as the curtain falls slowly on the second act.

At least, that's what was supposed to happen. And it would have, had I not, while he was sucking on my neck, opened one eye to see, up close and personal, this road kill in the middle of his forehead.

I tried not to laugh. And I didn't! However, when I hold back a laugh, I tend to – snort.

So the curtain fell slowly on this tableau: Dracula is feasting sensuously on Lucy's neck, while she, in her rapture, discharges a rapid fire succession of piggish snorts!

I prayed the crescendo of organ music would drown them out, or that the audience might mistake them for a creative take on an orgasm, and maybe it did. But the stage manager didn't, which is why, when the play ended, David and I bolted to our dressing rooms, changed, and fled the theatre. David didn't even take off his nose.

We had to move fast for two reasons. We didn't want the stage manager to catch us and give us the lecture we knew we deserved.

But more importantly, we had to make it back to my hotel room by midnight. Something a lot more dramatic than the play was happening that night.

But you'll have to wait for that one. I have a commercial audition early tomorrow. I'm trying out for "The Colon Lady."

My line – and this is no joke – is, "Hi there. Do you have gas, bloating, diarrhea?"

Betcha' can hear me snorting my way through that one!

Gotta go!

Big Squeeze,

Me

To: Margaret McNab
Re: *Mom and Her Royal Highness*

So Peggy, how was my colon lady audition, you ask? You are not going to believe this. I recited "gas, diarrhea and bloating" over and over this morning, until I could say it without laughing, then, when I got there, gave my sensitive, concerned read only to have the director stop me.

"What are you doing? You are the woman *with* gas, diarrhea and bloating! Your line, when asked the question, is, 'Yes, that's me!' You're not reading for the *colon* lady. We're bringing the colon lady up from LA."

A day in the life of a Canadian actor.

So, where was I? Oh yeah. David and I are racing to my hotel to catch the main event.

My dad was president of the Calgary Stampede that year. And, as you know Peggy, in Calgary, that's a big deal. It was an even bigger deal that year because the Queen and Prince Philip were on a cross Canada tour, and the Stampede was to be their last stop before they boarded their plane for England. Mom and Dad were their official hosts. Dad was to make a welcoming speech and presentation on stage in front of 17,000 people seated in the grandstand. Then, Mom, Dad, Liz and Phil were to take their seats in the Royal Box to watch the

Chuckwagon races. This event was to be broadcast across Canada and by satellite to England. The three-hour time difference would allow David and I to catch my Dad's speech live.

So, there we were, sitting on a creaky old bed in my firetrap of a hotel room, watching this fuzzy little TV screen. David was still sporting his plasticine nose and deranged eyebrows. We made it just in time to catch my father and mother greet the Queen and Prince Philip as they arrived in their horse-drawn carriage in front of the Stampede grandstand. The four of them mounted the stage, flanked by red-coated RCMP escorts. They all stood at attention as 17,000 people rose to sing "God Save the Queen." I was so proud of my parents, I started to cry.

Then, as silence fell over the crowd, my father, dressed like the cowboy he wasn't, stepped forward to the lectern, clutching the recipe cards on which he had written the speech that he had practiced for the past five months and was now going to make to her Royal Highness.

There was just one problem. It was a windy day.

As Dad took a breath to begin, his cards took flight like a flock of doves. The Mounties, holding tight to their Stetsons, ran around the stage, stomping on the fluttering pieces. Prince Philip started to laugh. My heart was in my mouth.

Then, Dad gave his best, and hugest, Jack Benny shrug and delivered his message. It was short and from the heart.

"Your Royal Highness, Prince Philip. You have been greeted all across Canada. You must be tired. So, I'm here to say good-bye. As a parent, I'm sure you miss your children and are eager to get back to them."

He presented the Queen with a white cowboy hat, symbolic of the Stampede, and a beautiful bronze statue of her favourite horse; one that the Mounties had given her years earlier.

Mom told me later that Philip turned to her and said, "Something more to go in the attic."

"Well don't tell George that!" Mom retorted. "He went to a great deal of trouble having it made."

I love my mom. She doesn't give two hoots if you are a king or a queen. If you deserve a scolding, you deserve a scolding.

Back in the hotel room, David carefully peeled off his nose. He was as impressed as I was proud. Here was this non-actor showing us all up. When his notes blew away, Dad didn't stand in front of 17,000 people and yell, "Fuck!" He didn't stand centre stage and snort either. The queen did. But then what do you expect? That woman has no control.

Nope. My dad dealt with it like a pro – even made something better of it. David let out a low whistle of admiration. "Your dad is one cool dude."

What he didn't know about – but soon would – was my mother.

After Dad's speech, the Mounties escorted Mom, Dad, Liz and Phil to the Royal box, which was draped with the bunting that you see at these events. I have to say that part of me was secretly relieved that the lower half of my mother's body was hidden from the view of the crowd and, more importantly, from the cameras that were broadcasting this event.

Now, my mother is a very elegant woman and has outstanding legs. But what you don't know, Peggy, is that all through my childhood and, to my complete mortification, as I struggled through my teens, she had this – problem. When she

75

sat down, she couldn't keep her legs together. This "legs apart" thing wasn't a form of exhibitionism on her part. Just a complete lack of awareness.

For instance, at a party, she'd get involved in telling a story or listening to someone else spin a yarn. If something funny was said, she'd kick up one leg in a show of enthusiasm then flop back on the couch.

At which point my father would say, "Sheila, put your legs together."

At which point she would huff, "They are together!"

And she really thought they were!

At one such party, when I was twelve and desperately trying to impress this thirteen-year-old boy, my mother was hooting away on the couch – girdle, garters and stockings on full display. I ran to the dinner table, grabbed a large linen napkin and threw it over her like a blanket.

"Thanks dear," she said, as she used it to dab tears of laughter from her cheeks.

So you can understand, Peggy, how relieved I was that Mom, Dad, and their new best friends were safely tucked away in the Royal Box, Dad's mini crisis over, and my mother's nether regions hidden from view.

The Chuckwagon races had begun, and the cameras moved in for a close-up of Dad and the Queen. She looked interested, which was pretty amazing considering the ceremonies she's had to witness throughout her career. In fact, she was laughing. Dad had the Queen laughing. Way to go Dad!

I started to relax.

The camera panned over to Mom and Prince Philip. I tensed a bit. Mom had suffered a crisis three months earlier.

I Paint Gophers!

Aside from the stress around the impending Royal visit, she had been very busy over the past two years, tagging along after Dad to his many functions as Stampede president. She had been playing the classic "wife of" role.

That April, I was in Calgary doing a radio show for CBC and, when it was finished, went out to the ranch to spend a few days. The first morning of my visit, still in my flannelette nightgown, I wandered into the kitchen in search of a coffee. My mother was at the kitchen table. She had been at the barn tending a sick horse and still had curlers in her hair. Her white shirt had a large brown stain of horse's cough syrup down the front. Her jeans were held up by a piece of binder twine from a bale of hay.

I started to say good morning then stopped dead in my tracks. Her face was ashen. She was clutching the edge of the table, staring straight ahead.

"Are you OK, Mom?"

"I can't breathe. My heart is pounding. I think I'm having a heart attack."

I panicked. We were thirty miles from help. I called Dad's law office in Calgary.

"Mom can't breathe. I think she's having a heart attack. Which hospital shall we go to?"

My father took control. "The General."

I raced downstairs to get dressed. When I returned, Mom was waiting at the front door.

"Bring me a clean shirt," she gasped. "I can't go to the hospital looking like this."

I grabbed one, then we sped into Calgary. I had one hand on the wheel and, with the other, tore the curlers out of her hair.

Eve Crawford

She wanted to look decent for the emergency ward.

Our family doctor was waiting. He whisked Mom behind a curtain to conduct a battery of tests. Some time later, he emerged.

"Her heart is fine. It's nerves. An anxiety attack. She hasn't been sleeping. I'll give her some Valium. You can take her home."

An hour later, Mom, Dad and I were sitting, side by side, on the front porch. The three of us stared ahead in silence. It was a warm early spring day. The leaves were starting to bud, and the Rockies, in the distance, were snow-covered. Dad, in the wisdom of his generation, had decided that gin would be better medicine than Valium, and the two of them were sipping martinis.

My father spoke first.

"Is it because of the Queen?"

"No, it's not because of the Queen!"

Dad tried again.

"I know what the trouble with you is. You don't think you're worth anything."

"Well I'm not! I haven't done anything with my life. All I am is married to you."

"Thanks a lot," said Dad.

"Mom, you've raised four of us."

"So what!"

Major silence as we all tried to work through that one.

Then Mom leveled a look at Dad and said, "And besides, you owe me $952,346.62."

"What for!"

"For all the things I've done for you over the last forty years.

I've been lying awake at night working it out, and that's what you owe me."

Dad looked appalled.

"What rate have you been charging?"

Then the three of us fell about, pulled back from the brink by the gods of laughter.

I don't know how, or if, my mother resolved this issue. My parents just celebrated their 65th anniversary. God knows what Mom's bill is now! I do know that at eighty-nine years of age, she is one of the brightest, funniest, toughest – and softest people I have ever known, and that I am blessed to have her as my mother.

And that is in spite of what she did that day in front of the queen.

So – where was I? Oh yes. Dad's got the queen laughing, things are going swimmingly there, and now the camera is on Mom and Prince Philip. Well, if I had worried about her nerves, I needn't have. She looked totally at ease. In fact, she was leaning back in her seat. Ok, I knew her legs were akimbo, but the bunting was doing the trick, where that linen napkin of years past had failed.

Though I couldn't hear what she was saying, I could tell Mom was explaining the Chuckwagon races to Prince Philip. At the same time, she was engaged in another habit of hers. When Mom gets engrossed in something, she twizzles her hair with her finger. Oh boy. I noticed a puzzled expression on Philip's face, as he leaned in to concentrate on what she was saying.

"What's happening?" asked David, plucking the final bits of brow from his forehead.

"She's not finishing her sentences! Her mind moves so quickly that she only offers tidbits of information. He's trying to fill in the blanks."

"What do you think she's saying?"

I translated.

"So when the horn – the outriders – oh boy there it – better make it quick – the driver takes off like a bat out of - in a figure eight. All the outriders have to – because if they – they're penalized – Oh! – that's the chick wagon out – in the pink – go! go! – yes! YES! Oh phew! Do you ride?"

And then it happened.

And it was nothing that the bunting could cover, and it was nothing that could be mistaken for anything else, and it was why the cameraman stayed with the shot, and why the CBC played it the next night on the National News.

My mother, while twizzling her hair, and speaking in broken sentences to the husband of the Queen of England, and in front of seventeen thousand people in the grandstand and anyone in Britain who chose to tune in – and we found out later that many did – took this opportunity to lean back and, with a slightly irritable look on her face, lift up her pelvis, clutch a huge chunk of her dress, and hike up her pantyhose!

"Your Mom is pulling up her pantyhose on national TV," intoned David.

As if I didn't know!

"Your mom is pulling up her pantyhose in front of the Queen," he said, awestruck. "She has got to be the most confident woman on the surface of the earth. Talk about 'What a woman's gotta do, a woman's gotta do.'"

Then, David paid the actor's all-time tribute.

"Eve, your Dad may be cool – but your Mom? She's Noel Coward!"

Well, Peggy, I guess this is the time, with all modesty, that I must say, "The leaves don't fall far from the tree."

It was a few years later that I managed to display the same cool, the same Noel Coward aplomb when, under desperate circumstances, I dealt with a crisis of my own.

The crisis of – Tim's penis.

But, it's late. So, I'll have to leave you hanging.

Har de har!
Eve

To: Margaret McNab
Re: *Tim's Penis*

Ok, Peggy. Just because you work in sexually transmitted diseases, you think any penis story of yours will trump mine? Pretty cocksure of yourself, Missy! Beat this one would you.

When I was thirty, I was in a Japanese disaster film called "Virus" – but that's another story. After it ended, I came down with a nasty virus of my own. Mononucleosis. Boy was I sick. I was covered in welts, couldn't eat and was barely able to move. As a nurse, you know there's no treatment but patience and long-term rest, right? But this wasn't just mono, Peggy. Along with it came a full-blown nervous breakdown. In those days, people didn't have depression, they had nervous breakdowns. Being unhappy was the norm for me. I didn't know there was another way to feel. It always struck me as odd, when I found out that other people didn't have at least one good cry a day.

So, I went home to heal. And there couldn't be a better place to do that than Mom and Dad's ranch in the Alberta foothills.

Now, a question might arise, and it would be a fair one. Why would I want to return to this place to heal? Well, for one thing, the lunacy that is my family makes all other pathology pale in comparison. But the other thing is the land. The West, like childbirth, is better experienced than described. The vast, sweeping skies brush the Rockies, the air is crisp, dry, crackling, and hawks do hang-glide over sun-bathed fields. I've seen it, breathed it. Like Chekhov's Madame Ranevskaya when she talks of her cherry orchard, "Oh my dear, my lovely, my beautiful orchard! My life, my youth, my happiness!" so my heart stirs every time my plane circles for its landing in Calgary. The landscape may be different. The attachment isn't.

The morning after I arrived, I was sitting at the breakfast table in my flannelette nightgown when it happened. The room started to spin. I could feel my skin prickle, my heart race and my mouth go dry, as wave after wave of terror swept over me. I staggered around the corner to the laundry room, where my mother was ironing a pair of underpants.

"Mom, I can't breathe."

She looked at me. Asked no questions. Didn't have to. She knew. She clicked off the iron.

"Let's get you dressed. Then we'll drive into the doctor's."

"But my appointment isn't until four."

"Doesn't matter. We'll just sit in his office until then."

She knew I had to be somewhere I would feel safe.

Then, she gripped my hand hard and led me downstairs to dress. I will always remember that grip. It was the only sensation I had. It was the only thing that separated me from the absolute certainty, that I was going to die, right there and then.

In a mirror image of our trip to Calgary seven years earlier, my mother drove me to the same doctor.

"Just an anxiety attack, your heart's fine," he told me.

My heart's fine? No, it isn't, I wanted to say. If it's fine, why do I lie awake at night composing inscriptions for my tombstone?

Here lies Eve Crawford - one big lump of potential

or

Eve Crawford - a life withheld

Why, at age thirty, do I lie awake at night wondering what I have done with my life?

But my mouth was too dry to speak.

The answers weren't to come right away. They never do.

But first, I had to get well. For two months, under the watchful eye of my parents, I did just that. I slept, I cried, I scratched, I gasped my way through my anxiety attacks until, little by little, I felt better.

Well – physically anyway.

But it took a strange event to set me on the road to emotional recovery.

On an August afternoon, the first day I had any energy, I decided to take my horse for a ride. I caught him in the field and started to lead him toward the barn, when I noticed he was moving very stiffly. His large brown eyes were dull and bewildered with pain. I felt the pang of alarm I now associate with my fear when one of my children becomes sick. He wasn't just a horse. He had been my best buddy and non-judgmental companion all through my teen years, when I was the gawkiest beanpole on the surface of the earth. He, on the other hand, was the most exquisite creature on the surface of the earth. A huge Anglo-Arab bay with a dished nose and the flexed head carriage typical of the breed, he was, in the horse world, what is known as a "good mover." Whenever he cantered, I felt as though I was in God's rocking chair, protected, soothed, and feeling kind of dozy.

And now he was sick.

I wrapped my arms around his neck.

"What's the matter with you, big fella?"

A damp sigh fluttered through his nostrils.

It was then that I saw Ike ambling down the road from the barn. Ike was our tall, lean, fifty-year-old ranch manager. Ike ran the ranch, because, as you know Peggy, my father is a lawyer not a rancher, and though Dad loved to toss around words like "hock," "heifer," and "filly," he had quickly figured out that ranching meant more than taking his bottle of Courvoisier through the spring blizzards to the newborn calves. Ike was one very important employee.

"Ike! Ike!" I called.

As he approached, he ceremoniously lifted his cowboy hat revealing a flash of white forehead – the mark of all true ranchers.

"Hello, Miss Eve."

Ike always made me feel as if I had walked right onto the set of "Gone with the Wind," so I always took him seriously.

"Ike, something's wrong with Tim."

I walked the horse back and forth. Ike looked down and fiddled with the rim of his hat.

"Looks like a *sheaf* infection."

"Sheaf?"

Visions of wheat swaying in the afternoon sun popped into my head – a beautiful picture from my grade-seven geography book – Chapter Four, "The Canadian West."

I searched his face for further clues. Ike had a creative way with the English language. He once told me he had a migrating headache.

When he heard my mother sing her excruciating rendition of "Somewhere My Love," I remember him saying, "Gee Mrs. Crawford, you've got such a pretty voice. You should sing with the Winnipeg Sympathy Orchestra. They play such lovely tunes. The 'Blue Damn You' is my favorite."

"A 'sheaf' infection? Ike, what's that?"

Well, Peggy, his sun-reddened face turned even redder. Even his forehead went pink.

"It's nothing I should be discussing with a lady, Miss Eve. You better call the vet."

"Oh - ohhhh!"

The penny dropped. A shea*th* infection. As in sword and sheath, as in not circumcised, as in – Tim's penis. I didn't ask another question. It would have been cruel. Ike looked ready to explode.

"Thank you, Ike."

I led Tim to the barn. I did not look back.

What did a sheath infection look like? I wondered, as I settled Tim into his stall. I quickly decided I didn't want to know. That's why God invented vets.

I hurried back to the house to place the call.

"I'll have Dr. Galeski call you when he checks in, but I wouldn't count on him today," said his receptionist.

I hung up. Tim would spend a night in pain. I had to do something.

Of course! Mrs. Chambers! After Mr. C. had died, she had moved to an acreage not far from our ranch. She knew everything. She would know what to do.

"Well darling, you're going to have to wash it."

"Wash it. Wash what?"

"The penis."

"How?"

"With a bar of soap. But it must be pure, dear. Ivory's the best."

I started to sweat. Maybe Mrs. Chambers would come over and do the job for me.

Oh come on, Eve. She's seventy. You're thirty. This is your horse. So what if you've lived in Toronto for ten years? You can do it.

But first – the question had to be asked.

"How, Mrs. Chambers – how do I make it – come down?"

"You rub it," she said briskly.

"Oh. Okay then. Well thanks Mrs. Chambers. Bye."

As I hung up the phone, I muttered, "Shouldn't be a problem. I wank off my horse every day."

"What dear?"

My mother had strolled into the kitchen. Hanging around her neck, on a bright red ribbon from last Christmas, were her very dirty reading glasses. Straight from her afternoon nap, she was headed to the kitchen table, where she would work on her crossword puzzle until she was fully conscious. As she settled in at the table, I considered asking her for help.

As you already know, Peggy, my mother is an extraordinary woman. What you don't know, is that in the 1930s she studied medicine, when very few women dared enter the profession. Her ambition, incredibly advanced for the time, was to teach birth control in India. Just one thing kept her from her dream. She was incapable of saying the word "penis."

Years ago, my sister Marti was visiting the ranch. She was

sitting on the front porch with Mom, having her morning coffee and a cigarette. Meanwhile, to mother's absolute horror, Marti's little boy, wearing nothing but a red plastic fireman's hat, was running around the yard. We had this flagpole on our front lawn, so of course he had to climb it and slide down, after which, he came wailing onto the porch clutching his crotch.

My mother, in her full *serves you right!* mode, said, "Oh dear, you've hurt your – *dooly*."

Marti, who was not a morning person, growled, "For God's sake, mother, it's called a PENIS!"

"Marti!" cried Mom, as she huffed and burbled her way back into the house.

Nope. Mother would not be the answer to my problem.

"Mom, do we have any Ivory soap?"

"I think so," came her distracted response. "Why?"

Maybe I was being silly. I had a grownup relationship with her now. I could say the word penis without having her recoil. After all, this was my horse I was talking about, not some guy I knew. This was animal husbandry. Nevertheless, I proceeded carefully.

"I have to wash Tim's penis."

"Arrrrrghhh!" she yelped, as she slapped her forehead. "Of course! P-e-n… penguin! Flightless seafowl! I was thinking ostrich, thinking flightless, not sea. Thanks dear. It's under the sink."

I eyed her. I'd sneak a look at the puzzle later on to see if she made all that up or just used what was on the page. Either way, she was good. She was very good.

So, I was on my own. I retrieved the bar of Ivory and a clean, pink cloth from under the sink, located the large tin pot that Mom had used to cook vegetables for all of my life, and filled it with warm water. Then, I grabbed the yellow rubber gloves by the sink and left for the barn.

What a relief! My father was mowing the lawn at the front of the house. I waved him down.

"Daaaaad!" I yelled over the roar of the lawnmower.

Beads of sweat were running down his face and dripping onto the ratty top of the long johns he always wore with his jeans. It made him feel like a farmer.

"Dad! Tim's got a sheath infection, and I have to wash his penis! Can you help?"

He cupped his hand behind his ear. "What dear?"

Years of legal negotiating had taught him to keep a straight face, but I was his daughter and didn't miss the slight bulging of his already large eyes.

"CAN YOU HELP ME WASH TIM'S PENIS!"

He gave me some old Navy salute and yelled, "Sure dear! I'll be with you in a minute!"

Then, he bobbed off over a hillock, and I didn't see him again until the next morning.

When I got to the barn, I realized I faced another obstacle. Tim had a phobia about being tied up. The job, sorry, procedure, would have to be done on this giant of a horse, as he stood untied in the middle of our barn. I led Tim out of his stall and positioned him in the center of the alleyway. I dropped the rope to his halter then hunkered down to get a view of the task at hand. The penis was out of sight, retracted into the sheath.

Ike was right. This was no task for a lady. Maybe I should wait for the vet. It was then that Tim turned his head, looked at

90

me and sighed. He was really sick.

For God's sake Eve, you're an actor. Pretend you're a vet! You are Dr. Quinn medicine woman – but for horses.

Fine! But how do I not get kicked from here to kingdom-come?

Then, the answer came to me. I poked my head out of the barn door to make sure not a soul was around. I returned to Tim and stroked his nose.

"Do you like Sinatra, Tim?"

He nudged me gently.

"I'll take that as a yes."

I snapped on the yellow gloves then squatted down at his rear end. He turned his head and gave me a quizzical look.

"I want you to just relax and enjoy this."

Then I began to croon and yes, my dear friend – stroke.

"Strangers in the night,

Exchanging glances,

Lovers at first sight,

Dooo doo dee doo dooo –"

I snuck a look at Tim. He was still looking at me, but his eyes were now at half-mast. So far so good! I sang on.

"What were the chances,

We'd be sharing love,

Before the night was thruuuuuu!"

Oh-my-god, Peggy! The penis descended. All of it!

I carefully scooped the bar of Ivory from the pot of water and, speed being of the essence, rubbed it quickly over the object at hand.

"Lalalalaloo – scrubscrubscrubscrubscrub – you'll get lots of oats, yesyesyesyesyes – and lots of crunchies tooooo."

91

I tossed the Ivory aside, grabbed the J-cloth, then rinsed away the lather. Hey, presto! All done!

Flushed with victory, I led Tim back to his stall. He looked ready for a smoke.

When I got back to the house, the phone was ringing. It was the vet.

"Miss Crawford? You've got a problem with your horse?"

"Hi Dr. Galeski. Yes, he's got a sheath infection."

"Do you have any antibiotics on hand?"

"Yes."

He gave me instructions on dosage and the number of shots to be administered, then said, "I'll still have to come over, though."

"Why?"

"I have to give him a tranquilizer."

"Why?"

"I have to prolapse the penis."

"Why?"

A note of irritation crept into his voice.

"I have to wash it."

"Oh, I've already done that."

"Did you get it all?" he asked, suspiciously.

"Oh yes," I yawned.

"It's twelve inches long you know!"

"Oh no, Dr. Galeski. It's a lot longer than that."

There was a moment's silence at the end of the line.

Then he said, "Well, I hope he sends you flowers."

I hung up then started to laugh, and I couldn't stop. And it wasn't just because of Dr. Galeski's unexpected retort. It

I Paint Gophers!

was because I felt something I hadn't experienced in a long time. It was joy. And it was then that I knew I was on my way. I was starting to heal. I was coming out of that deep, dark pit and into the light. I felt brave again.

Why? Because, Peggy, a girl who can wash her horse's penis – can do anything.

With love and hugs,
Eve

PART III

The Bad Mother's

Handbook

Calm before the storm

The storm

With Luke and Calvin

Boris Spremo

Meet Calvin

Meet Luke

One Woman's Guide to Disastrous Parenting

Introduction

Why on earth would anyone want to read a guide on parenting written by a bad mother?

Here's the truth: you have to spend years being a bad mother before you can be a good one, and by the time you are a good mother, it's too late. Damage done. In the hopes that it's not too late for you, I've decided to pass on some handy parenting tips. So you can throw out all those dust-ridden parenting books because, let's face it, we'd all rather kick back and read about serial killers.

In my thirties, I was dating my soon-to-be husband. I'll call him Ted. Ted and I were contemplating marriage but had a problem. I wanted to have children, and Ted did not. One night, we were out at dinner with my dad who was in town on business. Suddenly, Ted decides to run our problem by my father!

"Mister Crawford, Eve wants children, and I don't. You've raised four daughters. What's it like having kids? Is it nice?"

Dad took a swig of Scotch, put down his glass and said evenly, "Nice is not a word I would use, Ted." Then he went on a confusing ramble about how having kids had changed his life. This included learning how to ride a horse and moving to the country – a decision that, I recall, was made more on behalf of his two Labradors than his four daughters.

But Ted was an engineer. He needed measurement. He held his hands a foot apart and, looking at the space between them, said, "So basically, we're looking at a commitment from zero to twenty years."

Dad leaned across the table and said, "Oh no Ted. It neeeever ends!"

In spite of my father's caveat, Ted made the decision that it would be "nice" to have kids and suggested that we take the next step. If I had assumed that step was to get married, I was in for a bit of a surprise.

A few days later, we went out to celebrate my birthday at a nearby restaurant. We were joined by Ted's mother and his forty-year-old brother, Frank, who had been living in his father's basement for the past ten years, while he wrote his book on statistics – but that's a whole other story.

Ted's mother, Pixie, a petite woman in her mid-seventies, was into all things healthy. She routinely stashed zip lock bags of nuts and Rye Krisps in her purse. Whenever we invited her to dinner, she would bring her own meal to microwave. In between dainty bites of monochrome food, she would cast a reproving glance at the dinner I had served and say, "I hope you don't mind dear, but at my age, I have to be careful about what I eat."

One evening, I served prime rib. As I placed Ted's plate before him, Pixie pulled a pamphlet from her purse and slid it over to her son. The relevant bits were marked with pink highlighter.

"You might want to read this, Ted. If you knew what went on at those abattoirs," she said sweetly.

Then she gave me a pamphlet. "No need to read it now dear, but it might be of interest."

Highlighted in neon pink were these words.

"DO YOU SUFFER FROM VAGINAL ATROPHY?"

But, on my birthday night, as I looked at my future in-laws through the sepia lens of my second Manhattan, I felt relaxed and benign. Who cared if Pixie had ordered a salad – no dressing – to go with her sawdust crackers? Or if Frank was wagging his finger at me, telling me how much more writing I'd get done if I followed his disciplined schedule – you know, the one that had enabled him in ten short years to whip through to chapter two of his knee-slapper of a book on statistics. I had placed my subversive order for steak frites and was happily in the process of destroying my liver.

It was then that Ted leaned back in his chair and said, "Mom, Frank – Eve and I have an announcement to make."

Did we?

A horrifying thought struck me. Was Ted going to propose to me in front of his mother and brother? Please God, no!

"What?" asked his mother, all aflutter.

The waiter arrived with a basket of bread, and, just as he placed it in the centre of the table, Ted announced loud and proud, "Come September, I am going to unsheathe Mr. Happy!"

"Who's Mr. Happy, dear?" asked his mother.

The waiter left.

"Eve and I are going to have a baby," Ted beamed.

"Are you pregnant?" asked Frank. He was confused, as was everyone else in the restaurant.

"Not yet," explained Ted. He lowered his voice, and in an ominous tone, said, "First – Mr. Happy."

"Ohhhh," cried his mother, clapping her hands together in delight. "Well that's just wonderful!"

She rummaged in her purse to produce, yes, a pamphlet. Handing it to me, she said "It so happens, I brought this for you, dear. Just in case."

Highlighted in pink were these words:

DO YOU KNOW WHEN YOU'RE OVULATING!

Frank asked Ted, "Are you two getting married?"

"That depends on whether Eve can get pregnant. A lot of women her age have trouble."

Frank looked to me for comment. His expression was sad.

I was speechless. All I could do was drain my Manhattan.

A month later, I was pregnant. Once I got over three months of morning sickness, Ted and I married.

Now, if my vision of courtship and marriage had been a romantic one, so was my view of motherhood. It was not unlike those soft-focus pictures on condom boxes: a man and a woman walking arm in arm down a beach with one, and only one, kid perched on the guy's shoulders. Romantic and calm – a Trojan moment.

I was certain I'd be really good at raising kids. Why? I had raised and trained my horse, Tim. How tough could kids be? Feed them, groom them, pat 'em when they're good, and smack 'em when they're bad. Plus, as an actor, I had developed a grounding in psychology, improvisation and dealing with power struggles. Acting required enormous discipline, so I knew that whatever my kids threw my way, I would remain centred and calm. But best of all, acting had taught me to raise and lower my voice – without strain.

I would know exactly how to deal with child rearing issues such as sex education, spirituality, cleanliness, discipline and, most important of all, manners – something noticeably lacking in the children of my friends. I would sail through my labour without an epidural, breathe through my contractions – hee-hee-hee-hooo – while my admiring doctors confided behind their masks, "She's an actress, you know."

Soon after delivery, I would be fit, wear beautiful lingerie and return to my pre-kid libido. Lucky Ted. I would not let myself go, the way all those other women did.

Then I gave birth.

I felt as though a wrecking ball had hit my life, and, bit by bit, I had to assemble myself anew. I believe in God, in an undisciplined sort of way, but He has a wicked sense of humour. I grew up in an all-girl family, went to an all-girls' school. Boys were alien to me. So, God gave me two of them: Luke, followed four years later by Calvin. Of course, there was the sleep deprivation, the uncertainty and chaos of the babyhood years. But more confounding were the challenges I faced as the boys got older.

This handbook will offer some quick and easy tips for dealing with sex education, establishing boundaries, taking time for ourselves and, most importantly, how to manage the embarrassment or, as the English so delicately put it, discomfiture, in the face of our children's public behavior. As a matter of fact, let's start there.

Embarrassment

Who knew kids could be so embarrassing?

I know we are told to love them unconditionally but oh pooh! How many times have my kids made me feel like crawling into a hole? My horse, Tim, never made me feel like that. And I don't care about all those therapy sessions or Oprah quotes that tell me I'm responsible for my own feelings. Kids get to you!

Humiliation? I have earned my stripes in that department! I spent one New Year's Eve in emergency with my alcohol-poisoned fourteen-year-old, Calvin. What has my son getting drunk and ending up in the ER got to do with humiliation?

A friend had suggested that we go out that night to hear a mutual friend sing. I hadn't been out on New Year's since my divorce seven years earlier. I borrowed my neighbour's strapless, black, gypsy-style dress. To add dash, she had sewn a pink ruffle around the hem. I'd never worn ruffles in my life! To accessorize, she gave me her tiny pink purse, pink shawl and dangly pink earrings. I looked fabulous and fit for a Calypso at the Brazilian Ball – not that I'd ever been. Where was I going?

To the Pilot Tavern.

It was a start.

I admit I felt a little guilty leaving Calvin, but thought, he's fourteen! He was cozy and safe under my roof with three movies, two giant pizzas, and six of his dearest fourteen-year-old friends.

What could possibly go wrong?

I stayed at the Pilot until midnight, remained a polite half hour after "Auld Lang Syne," and then drove home through a blizzard. As I pulled into the driveway, I saw that the front door was open. Inside was chaos. The living room was filled with a bunch of adults I didn't know! They had been called in by Calvin's now-absent friends to look after my fourteen-year-old who was sprawled on the stairs, throwing up into a mixing bowl and weeping that he could no longer see! Paralyzed with terror, I sat next to him on the stairs. He clutched my arm.

"I love you Mom, I love you. I'm so sorry. I'm dying. It's not your fault."

I called an ambulance. Two paramedics sauntered in a few minutes later.

One of them looked at Calvin, still clutching the mixing bowl, and said, "So Calvin, would you like another drink?"

Calvin threw up blood.

At emergency, the admitting nurse asked him questions. He was in a wheel chair, and I was holding him upright by the collar of his shirt.

"What did you drink, Calvin?"

"Scotch, rye, Tia Maria, gin – "

She held up her hand. "That's enough!"

She sighed wearily, "God I hate New Year's."

Then her gaze fell on me. Her expression changed from weariness to disgust.

As I stood there in my ruffle-bedecked dress, holding my dry heaving fourteen-year-old in one hand, my pink party purse in the other, I could read the bubble over her head.

Bad mother, bad mother! Leaves her kid alone on New Year's Eve and goes out to party – in ruffles – pink ruffles.

Hot tears of shame dripped down my face. She was right. I was a ridiculous clown of a mother.

I have never worn ruffles since.

Public embarrassment? One December night, when Ted had the kids – we were divorced by then – I was lying on the couch, TV flicker in hand, reveling in my state of uninterrupted bliss when the doorbell rang. Two uniformed officers stood there. They asked if I had a twelve-year-old boy matching the description of my son, Luke. Two cops at your door? Your child is dead, right? As my legs gave way, they rushed to catch me.

"He's ok, he's ok! A woman saw him stealing her Christmas lights, and he also smashed the pumpkin on her front lawn."

Smashed a pumpkin? It's December for god's sake. Who's still got a pumpkin?

But the Christmas lights weren't so good.

Once I recovered from the shock of thinking Luke was dead, I was mad as hell. This was my night off, dammit! And he'd ruined it! I offered to ride with the officers to show them the way to his dad's. I wanted to be present, when these uniformed men gave my felon of a son official hell. I threw on my new coat, the one that made me look like an Inuit from Rosedale, and, head held high, did the "perp" walk down the sidewalk to the cruiser with its flashing lights. I could see the neighbours pretending not to look as they peeked through the slats of their Venetian blinds. Such amateurs. Didn't they know to turn the lights off first? The way I did when the cruisers were on their side of the street?

Yes, I have earned my stripes in the humiliation department. I have had endless chitchats with school principals and social workers, not to mention a very public, and embarrassing to this day, confrontation with some angry neighbours who objected to my skateboarder Luke's foul language and 24/7 occupation of our nearby intersection. These people seemed to think it had never occurred to me to tell Luke not to yell *fuck!* at the top of his lungs, when he pulled a "nutter." Or, to tell him to make way, politely, for cars – especially the police cruisers! My defense of my son that day, and, let's face it, my mothering skills, amounted to a shootout at the OK corral.

The day started with Ted and I taking a group of seven boys to a skate park for Luke's thirteenth birthday, finishing off with cake and candles on our front lawn. Ted then waved a merry goodbye, and left me with the seven boarders who had decided to stay on and skate the curb at the intersection. Two friends, Janet and Patty, joined me, and, together, we watched the kids buzzing back and forth like bees, gliding along the curb, doing their tricks and flips.

All of a sudden, a man from down the street marched over to the intersection with a bucket of sand and proceeded to dump it all along the curb.

Luke sped over to him.

"What the hell are you doing!" he shouted graciously.

I saw the man haul back his fist and, adrenaline being what it is, found myself, in the next instant, standing between the two.

Suddenly, three women materialized on the sidewalk, and they were all yelling at me.

One woman pontificated, "My son has ADHD and *he* doesn't behave like that."

"Well goody for you," I snapped.

Another woman, holding her baby girl, weighed in.

"I told your son the other day I was worried he'd get *killed* skating on the road like that."

"Really! His friend, Shitface, videotaped you saying you *hoped* he'd get killed!"

I looked at the baby in her arms.

"I hope your little girl doesn't give you trouble down the road, (I pray she grows into a Goth with eighteen rings in her nose) but if she does, I hope you have more understanding neighbours than I do."

"If my child gives me trouble, *I'll* deal with it," sniffed Miss Sanctimonious.

Then, this old bat from across the street, who was always having drunken brawls with her husband, chimed in.

"We're sick of your son swearing when he falls."

"Oh yeah! Well, all the people on this side of the street are tired of your foul mouth!"

At which point, birthday boy Luke, whom I thought had retreated to the house, pops his head over my shoulder and lips off, "Yeah, lady! So FUCK, FUCK, FUCK!"

At which point, I whirl around and slap him.

Everyone went silent.

I had never hit Luke in his life.

But did my neighbours know this? Their expressions of shock were quickly replaced by ones of smug satisfaction. No wonder the kid was a mess. He had an abusive mother.

I started to shake.

I felt a tug on my shirttail. It was Janet. She said calmly, "I don't think anything, at the moment, can be improved with discussion."

She took my hand and led me back to the house. I shuffled after her like an inmate from *One Flew Over the Cuckoo's Nest*.

Once inside, I started to sob. In between sobs, I took sips of gin kindly administered to me by my two friends. After I settled a bit, I felt a strange sensation on the left side of my face. My cheek had started to twitch! This could not be happening! I could not have a face twitch! I was scheduled to play a lesbian senator in two days. Bad enough I had to go with no make-up, but no make-up plus a face twitch?

"Where's Luke? Is he ok?" I choked, pressing my hand tight against my cheek.

"In the kitchen, having another piece of cake," Patty smiled.

"I can't believe I slapped him. I am so ashamed."

The tears started to spill again.

From the kitchen came a loud, contented belch.

Humiliation! In the end, it was my friends who came up with the answer.

As the two of them settled in on either side of me, Janet handed me a Kleenex and said, "Eve, have you and Luke thought of moving to Australia?"

"Right," said Patty. "They don't do embarrassment. Their nation was founded on bad behaviour."

Then, they put their arms around me and hugged me tight.

Sex Ed

I don't know how sex was explained to you, but I'll tell you how it was explained to me.

It wasn't.

At the age of ten, I asked my mother why my pony, Goldie, had to actually go visit the stallion to have a foal. Babies came when "two people are in love." Couldn't Goldie just stay at home and love him from afar?

My mother sat me down and gently explained Mendel's theory of breeding peas.

So, when it came time to explain sex, I was determined to give my boys the straight goods. What I wasn't prepared for was how early I'd be called upon. It started with Luke. At seven, he was going on at the dinner table about a girl in his class called Emma.

Through a mouthful of ketchup-covered fish sticks, he ranted, "I hate her. She is so sicketating!"

"Now Luke," I said, all June Cleaver, "what is so sicketating about Emma?"

Luke leapt from the table and, dripping contempt, gave a demonstration.

"She wears her hair in a ponytail with this ruffly elastic, and she wears skin tight leotards, and she – she – makes my pee pee move back and forth!"

I said nothing but, at a parent/teacher meeting later that week, I did tell Emma's mom to keep her little trollop of a daughter away from my son.

Shortly after the Emma tirade, Luke told me that, following his bedtime story, he didn't want me to kiss him goodnight on the cheek. He wanted me to kiss him on the lips.

I think Luke went through puberty at seven.

"No, no honey. Moms and boys kiss each other on the cheek."

I respected taboos.

That was until, on a rare night out, I shared this conversation with an actress friend of mine. She was French and expounded on my uptight nature and that of WASPS in general. In Europe, people kissed on the lips all the time: men and women, men and men, kids and parents.

I hated being called an uptight WASP.

When I got home, Luke swung open the door to greet me. He was wearing a balaclava and wielding a plastic sword. It was 11pm. Ted was asleep on the couch. I settled Luke into bed and read him a "Franklin the Turtle" story.

As I turned off the light, he pleaded, "Mommy, Mommy let me kiss you on the lips."

I thought about the Europeans. I wanted to be one – if only for a day.

"Ok Luke, but just this once."

He landed a big, sticky kiss on my lips. Then, in the half-light of the bedroom, his eyes widened in wonderment.

He stood up on the bed, looked down at his pajama bottoms, and exclaimed, "Whoa Momma! My pee pee growed!"

I fled down the hall.

Filthy Europeans!

But the real challenge came a few weeks later, when Luke was home for lunch. I was making tuna sandwiches. He was sitting at the kitchen table playing with his Batman and Robin figures.

"Mom, what is sex?"

"Do you really want to know, Luke?" I asked, playing for time as I buttered the bread.

"Yes, yes I do."

Mendel's theory or the No-Frills version? I went for it.

"Well Luke…"

I threw a blob of mayo into the tuna.

"… sex, is when a man and a woman get together, and they like each other a lot, and…"

I mushed the mayo and tuna together.

"…well, they love each other and hopefully are married and… "

I spread the tuna then slapped on the other piece of bread.

"…and they kiss a lot…"

I put the sandwich in front of Luke. He took a big bite.

I turned back to the sink and, keeping it casual, said, "Then, the man puts his penis into the woman's vagina."

Silence.

I started to wash a dish.

More silence.

I turned to look at Luke. He was staring straight ahead, chewing deliberately. I couldn't read him. Had he heard me?

"Luke?"

At last, he swallowed. Then he turned to me.

"Mommy – does Daddy do that to you?

113

"Yes, yes he does, Luke."

He shook his head sadly.

"You must have an awful life."

Needless to say, I was pretty discouraged over my botched attempt at sex ed but consoled myself with the thought that it might keep Luke celibate and safe a few years longer than most kids. Describe it, and they won't do it. Aversion therapy.

However, in my selfish desire for grandchildren, I chose not to explain sex to Calvin. Let him learn it on the street, the way I did. Or – Luke could fill him in.

What was I thinking?

One night, shortly after Ted and I separated, the kids were spending the weekend at their father's. Luke, now twelve, called me from Ted's apartment to tell me he was doing his homework at his dad's desk and had been searching the drawers to find a marker.

"And guess what I found Mom?"

"What?"

"A six pack!"

"Of beer?"

"No! Of condoms!"

"Oh."

"And guess what? Two were missing!"

I reassured him in my sweetest fake voice, "Well sweetie, it's nothing to get upset about. But there are some things you're not supposed to see, so it might be best if you don't say anything to anyone else about this, including your dad. It's kind of private."

I hung up and patted myself on the back for being such a wonderful mother and a really good ex-wife.

The next evening, when the kids came home, sugared up and bursting with boy energy, Luke whirled on his seven-year-old brother.

"Calvin! I forgot! You'll never guess what I found in Dad's office drawer!"

"Luke!" I warned.

"What? What!" shouted Calvin.

"Luke, no! We talked about this!"

"Condoms!" exclaimed Luke.

Calvin's jaw dropped.

Luke eyes narrowed, as he went in for the kill.

"And guess what? Two were missing!"

Calvin's eyes widened in outrage.

"What a rip off!"

Calvin's next episode of "Learning it on the Streets" occurred when our neighbours had their first baby – a boy.

On a July evening, a bunch of us mothers had gathered in front of my house. Our huge driveway, complete with basketball hoop, had become the unofficial community centre for the "hood." Sitting in a semicircle of plastic Muskoka chairs, we formed a barricade that served to trap the kids in the driveway, so they wouldn't run onto the street. As they shot hoops and rode their trikes, we knocked back beers and gossiped while keeping our kids safe at the same time.

A woman in our group had just delivered a present to the couple for their newborn.

"Dan and Jess are having a big fight," she reported.

"Why?" asked one woman.

"Apparently, Dan doesn't want to have the kid circumcised."

115

"But Jess is Jewish. You'd think they'd have that sorted out by now," said another.

I stretched, took a swig of my Heineken, and yawned, "Well it could be worse. The kid could have been a girl, and they could live in Africa."

At which point, all the women crossed their legs.

"Eeeyouuu! Eve!"

The next morning, Calvin, his mouth stuffed with Cheerios, asked, "Mommy, what happens to little girls in Africa?"

"You don't want to know honey."

"Yes, I do."

Calvin could be relentless, so I took a deep breath and said, "Well, in some countries in Africa – and there are organizations all around the world trying to stop this – they cut off the part of the girl that is like the boy's penis, but smaller. It's called the *clitoris*."

Calvin let out a gasp and covered his mouth.

"Oh Mommy!"

"I know it's awful. Let's not talk about it."

Then he said, "*That's* a clitoris?"

I was confused. "Yes."

"Oh no! I thought a clitoris was a girl's bum, and yesterday in class, when I went to sharpen my pencil, I told Rebecca to get her clitoris out of my way."

I kept my voice calm.

"What did Rebecca say?"

"Nothing. She just moved."

"Did Monsieur Fontaine hear?"

"No."

Phew! They were clamping down big time on sexual harassment in the schools these days.

Gently, I said to Calvin, "Now that you know what it *is* sweetie, it's probably not a good idea to use that word for another twenty years, ok? You know what? Maybe never."

So how do you teach your kids about sex?

You don't.

Let the school do it.

Setting Boundaries

Setting boundaries is a tough one. First, you have to know which boundaries to set.

Do you let them play with toy guns? Not me. Though Luke managed to work his way around that every morning, when he chewed his toast into the shape of a gun and shot me as I cleaned up the kitchen.

What to let them watch on TV? Do you allow them to watch Ninja Turtles then go on to karate kick the kids at preschool? Shows about beloved family pets? That should be ok.

Not so fast.

One morning, in my rush to get Luke to school, I was brushing my teeth with one hand and applying eyeliner with the other. Luke stood at my side riveted to his image in the mirror. He had worked the globs of toothpaste in his mouth into a massive amount of white foam and was now letting it all drool out of his mouth, down his chin and onto his clean, morning shirt. I lost it.

"Luke! What are you doing?"

"I want to see what I'd look like with rabies," he slobbered.

Was I wrong to let him watch Old Yeller or Cujo?

How do you make kids apologize? Can you really make someone say sorry and mean it? Luke came up with a creative and face-saving solution to this dilemma that I still use to this day. At three, he had a kid over for a play date, and, for some reason, decided to whack the boy on the head with his plastic bat cave. I sent him up to his room and told him he couldn't come down until he said sorry. Ten minutes later, stressed out that his friend had unhindered access to Batman, Robin *and* the bat cave, he inched halfway down the stairs on his bum and looked at me through the railing.

I looked up at him.

"Well?" I said, hands on hips.

"I just want to say a *little* bit of sorry."

Karate kicks, bat caves, rabies drool; how innocent, how sweet those problems seem now.

One post-divorce day, I was in a story conference for a soap opera. We writers were seated around a large, round table. We were laughing our faces off. It was one of those joyous times, when you are with your "tribe" doing what you love most in the world – making up stories about people, gossiping about them without guilt, and getting *paid* for it!

At this meeting, we were trying to figure out who would be revealed as the father of Tiffany's baby. Tiffany couldn't tell anybody. Tiffany was in a coma. This was due to her lack of chemistry with the leading man. The producers didn't kill her outright in case viewers complained about her absence, in which case, they'd revive *her*, and kill off the boyfriend instead.

We were batting about the possibility of Tiffany's obstetrician, Dr. Fukasaku, being the father. What a great, episode-ending scene to have Fukusaku, as he whisked the newborn over to the scales for its APGAR rating, notice the resemblance, take a beat to register his astonishment, then mask his surprise and continue the examination.

We broke for coffee. I made the mistake of checking my messages. There was one. It was from the principal of Luke's junior high school. She had suspended him for skateboarding down the railing of the nearby UNICEF building, after which he sprawled on the hood of a cab and squished his face, cross-eyed and drooling, against the windshield while his friend and videographer, Shitface, recorded this as part of a bigger project called "Luke's Life."

My stomach knotted at the news. Tomorrow I would have to face another swell chat with the grim-faced principal.

When I returned to the conference table, I was a preoccupied wreck. Who cared if Doctor Fukasaku was the father of Tiffany's baby? Who cared if the producers had to kill off the infant soon after birth, because kids were too hard to work with? I had to deal with my own kid – figure out what I was going to say to him, what punishment I could mete out that wouldn't punish me.

By the end of the day, I had no answers. All I could do was stop at the beer store on the way home. As I marched up the front steps clutching my six-pack, the front door swung open.

My gangly thirteen-year-old, his voice loud and cracking, protested, "Yo! It wasn't my fault! That Mrs. Swenson is so gay!"

I shoved by him and, bottles clinking, headed directly to my bedroom, locked the door, got into bed, twisted the top off the first beer and chugged it down.

Luke, all the while, was thumping at my door as he yelled, "It wasn't my fault! Oh my God! It's none of her business what I do on my lunch hour. Besides, that railing is public property, and that cab driver? I didn't even dent his hood!"

I cracked open another beer, reached for one of my dust-covered parenting books and flipped madly through the index looking for "school, suspension from..."

Didn't find anything that helped. But the beer did. Then, I noticed another book. "The Man Who Listens to Horses." I leafed through it, as I sipped my second beer. Luke's protestations became more distant and far less bothersome.

Finally, I got up and swanned out of my room. Luke, at this point, was sitting slumped on the floor in the hallway.

He leapt up to continue his tirade, but I held up my hand like a crossing guard and said, "I don't care why you were suspended. I don't want you to *look* at me or *talk* to me, until *I* talk to you. You will stay inside all day tomorrow, and there will be no TV."

Imperious, I flicked my fingers at him. "Now go away."

He was nonplussed. Where was his hysterical mother?

The "Horse Whisperer" was right on! I was the angry mare kicking my colt out of the herd. And he wouldn't be allowed back in until he had curried plenty of favour. He had to figure things out for himself. I sure couldn't. One day he would grow up.

Until then – I would drink.

On the subject of setting boundaries, I have talked mostly about Luke. Did Calvin require fewer limits, or was I simply too tired to set them? During my separation and divorce, preoccupation, plus super fatigue, left me a little lax in the boundaries department.

When he was eight, Calvin watched a lot of horror shows. He loved them. He didn't have any nightmares, was doing well in school and seemed to be a well-balanced kid, so I rationalized that he was the next Stephen King.

Though one day at the video store, I reached my nadir in the parenting department. Calvin came over to me clutching two videos.

"What have you got?" I asked.

"'Slumber Party Massacre' and 'Office Killers,'" he chirped.

"Ok then! Let's go!"

As I turned toward the checkout, I caught a man over at "New Releases" looking at me, his face awash in judgment.

I'll show you, I thought. I snatched one of the tapes from Calvin and said loudly, "You are *not* renting 'Slumber Party Massacre!'"

"Why!" he protested.

"Because you've watched way too many movies with naked women being chopped to bits!"

The man took out his phone. Was he calling Children's Aid?

"Please Mom – pleeeeze!"

"Absolutely not! 'Office Killers' and that's it!"

I tossed the guy a superior glance. *See! I have my standards!*

On the subject of setting boundaries, the "Horse Whisperer" has it nailed.

1. Establish who is leader of the pack. (that would be you!)
2. When the colt/kid misbehaves, boot him out of the herd until he's willing, through good behavior, to "join up" again.
3. Affect a calm assertiveness with the odd bit of compromise thrown in. (That would be "Office Killers.")

Taking Time for Ourselves

I read an article on parenting that emphasized how important it was to *take time for ourselves*. So, I decided to give myself a pedicure. I bought all the necessary goop and appliances at the drugstore, including a fabulous hot pink nail polish by Opi, a company known for inventive, often hilarious, names for its colours.

The presenting problem was how to occupy the kids while I beautified. I decided to rent them a video, but it would have to be one that engaged them both. I felt a bit guilty about the crap Calvin had been watching, so, in an effort to upgrade the horror, rented Stephen King's "Carrie." I hadn't seen it since its 1970s release, but remembered it was gripping and had a terrific inferno at the end. That gave me pause, but then I thought there was an inferno in "Bambi," and *it* was family rated.

"Carrie" should buy me some time.

That night, I fed the kids their fish sticks, slipped in the video, then went upstairs to work on my toes. Lost in the bliss of uninterrupted thought, I soaked my feet, trimmed cuticles and pumiced calluses. Then, as I started to apply the first coat of pink, my head snapped up. Something wasn't right.

The silence.

Regardless of how good a movie was, there was always some bickering going on between the boys. Kleenex entwined between my toes, I crab-walked on my heels halfway down the stairs and peered over the railing to see what was happening.

Full frontal nudity was happening, that's what was happening! Sissy Spacek was cowering in the shower, while a bunch of girls threw tampons at her! The boys were motionless, rapt. Oh god!

Then I thought, *well too late, nothing I can do now, they've already seen it.* So, I hobbled back upstairs and finished my toes. It was then I noticed that the colour by Opi was called, "You're a Piece of Work."

The next morning at breakfast, Calvin, who struggled with his th's at the time, confided, "Mommy! Der were *veeeginas* in dat movie last night."

I slumped. Someone really should call Children's Aid.

"I know honey. I forgot. I never should have let you watch it."

He patted my hand reassuringly.

"It's ok Mommy. Dey covered 'em up wiff hair."

What is it that makes taking time for ourselves so hard? Is it guilt? If so, does our guilt serve our survival?

Rarely.

So paint your toes dammit!

But lay off the ruffles.

Conclusion

In spite my unfortunate mothering techniques, there have been moments along the way that tell me, somehow, my boys will survive.

Calvin, in spite of his exposure to *Slumber Party Massacre* and *Office Killers*, developed a true sense of romance. At ten, he told me one night that his best friend, Jacob, had taken a girl out on a noon-time date, and, not to be outdone, he had asked Debbie, a girl he really liked, if she would go on a lunch date with him.

"She said yes! Oh Mom, I want to buy her a rose? Only, it costs two bucks! Would that be too *exquisite* of me?"

"It would be very exquisite of you. But Calvin, you can never go wrong being exquisite."

When he came home the next day, I asked him how it went.

"I didn't buy her a rose because Jacob had already given *his* girlfriend a rose. So instead, I bought her a bag of candy, took her for a slice of pizza, and then we went back to school and promised each other *we would never talk about it.*"

Debbie's mother described her daughter's version of the date.

"We just talked," said Debbie.

"What did you talk about?"

With a world-weary sigh, Debbie said, "Oh Mommy, we've known each other since *kindergarten*! We just – reminisced."

As for Luke, in spite of his monosyllabic, rabies-drooling defiance of the status quo, he showed glimmers of the insightful, fiercely honest young man who has emerged today.

One night, as I tucked him in, I was explaining the difference between an optimist and a pessimist.

"I think I'm in between," he said.

"How come?"

"Cause I'm going to be a big time NHL player – better than Gretzky!"

Luke was playing house league hockey at the time.

"Wow! I'd call that optimistic."

"Yup. I'm going to score *fifty* hat tricks a game."

"Whoa! You're not an optimist, Luke. You're a megalomaniac."

"What's that?"

"Someone who thinks they're God."

He wrinkled his nose.

"Who'd wanna be God?" God can't skate faster than Gretzky."

I saw a teaching moment and went for it.

"Yes Luke, yes He can. *God* can skate faster than *anyone*."

He shook his head.

"No way! God wears sandals!"

My two unique and polar-opposite boys have been both my biggest gift – and greatest challenge. But this much is certain: They have raised me far more than I have raised them. They have "grown me up," and their work isn't done yet. Not by a long shot.

As parents, we must never forget that, first and foremost, we are human. And because we are human, our resources are finite. It is often against all odds that we still *show up*.

Once, when I was despairing over a problem I was having with one of the boys, a wise friend told me "Sometimes in life there *are* no solutions – only choices."

But making these choices can be painful and full of uncertainty. Knowing when to set limits or when to give up control takes courage and, ultimately, a leap of faith.

The best advice I have ever had on parenting came from my eighty-two-year-old father. One of the boys was really struggling, and I needed guidance.

"Dad, how do you motivate a kid?"

His answer surprised me.

"You don't. You discipline them, you love them – and then you pray."

So, in the end, we do what we can do. And then, we hand it over – to the Guy in the sandals.

PART IV

Rice Christians

Cookies and Christ

I decided to go church again when my boys were three and seven. I did this for two reasons. First, the church was across the fence from our house, and even though it was United and I was an Anglican, location, location, location won out. The second reason was that my friend Meredith, a fellow, beleaguered mother of two boys, told me that free babysitting was available during the service. The thought of a kid-free hour on a Sunday morning was sublime: an opportunity for me to slide down in a pew and gaze into the middle distance. An added bonus was that United Church parishioners don't have to stand as much as Anglicans do; nor do they have to kneel. They just slouch forward when they pray – another opportunity for uninterrupted sleep.

The following Sunday, Ted and the kids and I went to our first service. The minister's name was Bob. He was in his mid-forties, had a scraggly beard, florid complexion and crooked yellow teeth. He introduced himself and his portly wife, Mavis, at coffee hour, as elderly ladies in floral dresses served coffee and Dare cookies to the congregation.

One Sunday, my parents, on a visit from Calgary, accompanied us to church. Dad watched the adults sip and chat, while the little kids wormed their way through the big people to the trestle table, where, with grimy hands, they grabbed handfuls of cookies.

"Rice Christians," he harrumphed, referring to the Christians' history of bribing the heathens into church by promising them rice, or cookies, or, in my case, a nap.

For the next two years, the church became an extension of our home. We enrolled three-year-old Calvin at a Montessori school there, both boys used the church grounds and gymnasium as their playground, and I served on all sorts of committees. I was also recruited, from time to time, to write and deliver the sermon. I made friends with many of the other moms, and, in getting to know the elders of the congregation, stopped thinking they all looked alike.

Because I was an actress, Reverend Bob enlisted me most Sundays to read the lesson. I took this task seriously, because most of the congregation was hard of hearing, and many told me at coffee hour that it had been years since they had actually heard the reading. Also, because I knew so little about the Bible, I did my best to understand the message and its greater context.

One Saturday night, close to Christmas, while grappling with a reading that involved God the Father, God the Son and God the Holy Spirit, I decided to call my parents in Calgary. I wanted to check in, but, more importantly, I wanted to tell them I was reading the lesson. At forty-five years old, I was still seeking their approval and wanted them to know, that on top of having two children at an advanced age while continuing my so-called career, I was also on my way to becoming a God-fearing woman.

Dad answered the phone. He and Mom were in the kitchen

and, after way too many drinks, were fighting over how to cook the peas. They ate peas with every meal and, therefore, had had this fight every night of their fifty-five-year marriage. I told Dad about the reading.

"That's nice, dear."

Then, he said to Mom, "Sheila, don't put those peas in yet! Wait for the water to boil. Have you salted it?"

"Yes, I've salted it!" I heard her snap in the background.

Mom, who downed three dark-colored rye and waters before every meal, would regularly pick up Dad's Scotch by mistake, knock back half of it, then screw up her face in disgust to announce, "That's not my drink."

So, by the time dinner rolled around, she was mean, hungry and ready, at that point, to gnaw through the bag and consume the peas in their frozen state.

I tried to regain Dad's attention. "Dad, I need your help here!"

"Yes, dear."

"I think I get who God is, and who Jesus is, but who, exactly, is the Holy Ghost?"

There was a pause at the end of the line.

"Well – isn't he the one who impregnated Mary?"

"Mary! Mary who!" gasped Mom in the background.

"Oh for Christ's sake, Sheila! No one we know. Mary, mother of Jesus!"

"Don't be so stupid," she spat back. "The Holy Ghost did not impregnate Mary!"

"Well who did then? The peas, the peas!"

I struggled to get back in the conversation.

"Maybe it was Joseph! In which case – Christmas is cancelled. Ho, Ho, Ho!"

Eve Crawford

But they were gone. It was suppertime, and for my parents, dinner, and much of life for that matter, came down to the peas.

Now, if going to church was about my longing for sleep, I soon discovered that the experience called upon me to wake up: to give back, to learn about the Scriptures, to think about life.

But before I get too grand, I must admit that what I loved most were the people who attended. Our neighbourhood was the epitome of white bread, middle-class Toronto. People were polite, dutiful, and, well – Canadian. Nothing outrageous ever happened. Or so I thought. However, I soon discovered that all the houses in the area with their thoughtful gardens, tidy lawns, and neat front porches were like an Advent calendar, the one with little doors and a piece of chocolate hidden behind each one. But in this case, instead of chocolate, there was something way more delicious.

There was scandal!

And our church was frequently at the center of it.

Hilda, the choir mistress, fascinated me. A square-built woman, she wore long, flowered dresses, reverse heel clogs, no make-up and pinned her long strawberry-red hair into a tight bun – your basic Mennonite look. She accompanied herself on the guitar, as she sang in a high-pitched, reedy voice. On Sundays, when I had one eye open, I would fantasize about doing a makeover on Hilda; a little eyeliner, let the hair down, lose the clogs. We'd deal with the dress after she lost a few pounds. But, just as I was settling on her new look, Reverend Bob announced one Sunday that Hilda was leaving the church to do her PhD in music.

Damn. Too late for the do over.

I Paint Gophers!

I didn't give Hilda much thought until, three months later, while striding down Yonge Street, I glanced at a full-page picture of a woman's face staring out at me from the Toronto Sun box. I lurched to a stop, threw some coins into the machine and grabbed the paper. There was Hilda, face clean-scrubbed, hair still in a bun.

Over her forehead, the headline screamed –

"WOMAN ARRESTED FOR STALKING U of T PROF"

Apparently, Hilda had been obsessed with her French professor of twenty years past and had been periodically stalking him for the last two decades. It was only when she tried to abduct his daughter from private school that the police moved in for the arrest.

Our choir mistress!

I was humbled. There I had been for the last two years, sitting in the second pew smugly judging the book by its cover, when, all along, under that flowered tent dress, was a woman seething with desire, planning and plotting and, ultimately, letting nothing get in the way of the object of her lust. Well, except for the police.

Yes, yes, I know the situation was tragic for all parties involved, but I have to say the heathen in me was thrilled. On the other hand, what fun would church be now with Hilda incarcerated!

Little did I know, things were to get even livelier.

Hilda's replacement was Barbie, a pert, fresh-faced, Peter Pan of a woman, who wore short skirts and wore them well. Soon after she joined our church, Barbie assembled a kick ass choir that really started to rock the place. She also started to

137

rock Reverend Bob. Reports flooded in from harried mothers who, in the midst of herding their kids to school, had spied Bob and Barbie sweat-drenched and crimson-faced, jogging through the neighbourhood every morning.

Bob started boasting, to anyone who would listen, about how much weight he was losing. One day, I witnessed him refusing to buy a box of Girl Guide cookies from an eager, toothless, seven-year-old Brownie.

"Oh no. I can't buy those cookies," he said, patting his diminishing pot. "I'm on a diet."

As the little girl's face collapsed along with her sale, I wanted to say, "Just buy the fucking cookies, Bob."

But, because I had been a Brownie in my day, I would never use such language.

Now, as Bob lost weight, his wife Mavis gained it, and, as they say in the horse world, she was already a good doer. Church was becoming ever more interesting. Instead of falling asleep during the sermon, I started to watch for telling body language between Bob and Barbie and Mavis who, by the way, sang in the choir conducted by Barbie!

What was going on? we women mused at coffee hour, as we huddled in our bitchy little circle, chomping on our cookies.

"Maybe nothing. Maybe a jog is just a jog."

"As if!"

Another woman confided, "I heard Mavis kicked Barbie during the church soccer game."

"Is that why she's limping?"

All this only fifteen minutes after the sermon. Boy, church wore off fast!

A few weeks later, everyone in the congregation got a letter calling us to a meeting in the church gym. We were advised to make babysitting arrangements, as the subject matter was not meant for little ears. Apparently, Barbie had lodged a complaint with United Church headquarters claiming Reverend Bob had "breached his fiduciary power" by enticing her to pound the Posturepedic with him – or words to that effect. Head honchos from the United Church had been called in to run the meeting. In days of yore, this was known as a "public hanging."

Well! If Reverend Bob had worried about the shrinking numbers of the congregation, he needn't have. The turnout, that warm night in May, was bigger than Christmas and Easter combined. As Ted and I passed the magnolia tree at the entrance to the church, I envisioned a noose looped over one of its branches. The Salem witch-hunts came to mind. But this wasn't Colonial Massachusetts; it was mid-town Toronto at the turn of the millennium. Could it get any better?

Yes, it could!

Inside the gym, the trestle tables were set up, and, in keeping with church tradition, the ladies' auxiliary was out in full force serving coffee and Dare Cookies! We got to sip and munch, while we listened to Bob and Barbie tell their respective stories of adultery.

Wooden chairs had been lined up in rows, with an aisle created down the middle. Seated at the front, behind a table, were four church officials conferring with one another, as they sifted through thick dossiers. We all got our goodies then took our seats.

The meeting was called to order by a sixty-something woman wearing, yes, a floral dress. Speaking into the table mic, she laid down her agenda in the soft, calming tones of a kindergarten teacher settling her kiddies on their mats for an afternoon nap. Barbie and Bob were each going to speak – then leave the room. After that, members of the congregation were invited to share their pain with the church leaders and with each other.

Pain? I stopped chewing. I was halfway through my Caramel Chip cookie. Was I supposed to be in pain? I glanced furtively at the people nearby. Most of them politely sipped their coffee but had the good grace to save their cookies for later. It occurred to me that maybe this was serious, that this wasn't a soap opera but real people's lives. Then I saw Bob's wife, Mavis, in the front row, her ashen face a profile in stone. Ashamed of my prurient interest, I tried to chew quietly. Next to me, my friend, Meredith, had no such compunction. She chomped away, spraying crumbs in all directions.

Raising boys reaps havoc with your manners.

Barbie took the mic at the front. In a quaking voice, she told of coming to work at the church, of how Bob was not only her employer but also her spiritual counselor. That she had been suffering from depression and went to him for guidance. That he reminded her very much of her father and – let's get Freudian – she found him attractive. Bob shared with her that he too was depressed and, in doing so, had pressed her "nurturing" button.

"Not the only button he pressed," spat Meredith through her Chocolate Chunk Dare.

I started to shake. I could have killed Meredith. Just when I was feeling all compassionate! In an effort to control myself, I leaned forward, cupped my hands around my eyes and focused hard on the linoleum squares beneath my feet. People glanced solemnly in my direction. They thought I was weeping.

In a quaking voice, Barbie continued.

"We began our relationship, and, though I felt guilty, Reverend Bob assured me that our union was blessed by God."

"Gawd!" guffawed Meredith.

A chunk of chocolate landed in my lap.

I pressed my lips together and squeaked. Again, people looked in my direction.

Oh dear, Eve is taking this harder than Mavis! She is so sensitive.

Ted, on the other side of me, was upright and attentive and taking notes!

Barbie finished her testimony, then Bob took the mic.

He suddenly transformed into Clarence Darrow, as he addressed "we the jury."

"To point one, I say yes! To point two, I say yes! But to point three, I say an emphatic no! Our relationship was consensual!" he boomed.

Then he took his seat.

At this point, a man on a walker, accompanied by an elderly church lady, made their way down the aisle. In unison, they gave Bob and Barbie a solemn nod. The two sinners got up and were escorted by their handlers out of the gymnasium to separate rooms in the basement, where they would wait for the head brass to deliver their verdict.

The chairwoman then proceeded to address us in her treacle-coated, over-enunciated voice.

"This can't be easy for any of you, so we want to offer you this opportunity to share your pain. But, there is to be no blame. We are not here to judge Bob or Barbie. Please use the mic, so everyone can hear you, and remember to use the 'I' word when you speak. Now – who would like to share?"

141

Dead silence.

I took this opportunity to bite into the other half of my cookie. The crunch was deafening. A woman in the row ahead turned and glared at me. I stuffed the piece into my right cheek, stared at my lap and tried to disappear.

More silence.

And then – my worst nightmare. Ted stood up.

"I would like to speak!"

He always affected a phony, deep voice when speaking in public or, oddly, talking to another male. It was his version of chest beating.

"Yes," chirped the chairwoman in relief. At last – a sensitive, hurting soul ready to unburden his pain.

"The way I see it is –"

But the chairwoman interrupted. He had broken the first rule.

"Please, take the mic."

"No need!" boomed Ted, proudly. "I am a university professor. I know how to project."

"But –"

Ted pressed on.

"The way I see it is this. We have a great church here, and we don't want to ruin it. So how 'bout we settle things right now. I say we take a vote. Who's for Bob, and who's for Barbie?"

The chairwoman turned ashen.

"No, no! We are not here to judge. And please, use the 'I' word."

Ted looked confused. "But I just did. *I* say we take a vote."

I regarded my husband during the incredulous silence that followed. He was an engineer, and his linear thinking often produced solutions that were so simple-minded that they actually had their own idiot savant sense.

I Paint Gophers!

Then all hell broke loose. People started arguing, making their case for one sinner versus the other. No one used the mic or the "I" word, and the chairwoman's voice was quickly drowned out in the din. One man loudly proclaimed that Bob had kept him from committing suicide, and, therefore, the church should keep him on. A ninety-something man said that Bob was wrong to do what he did, but, let's face it, Barbie's skirt lengths were a temptation too great to resist, at which point, his ninety-something wife yanked him back into his seat. Meredith loudly weighed in that she cared less about Barbie's skirt lengths but seriously questioned her taste. How could she kiss a guy with such bad teeth? People in the row ahead whirled on her. She held up both hands.

"Just sayin'."

When the dust settled, Bob got suspended for a three-month unpaid leave and was ordered to go for therapy. He was later reassigned to a parish in Orangeville. Barbie married her new boyfriend and moved to England. I quit going to church to focus on my divorce proceedings.

🌱

In the fall of that year, I took Calvin to his new school for senior kindergarten. One of the young moms from church was there.

"Who's the new choir mistress?" I asked.

"Oh – no *mistress*! We aren't risking that again. It's a guy, and he's terrific."

A month later I saw the same woman on the playground.

"How's the choirmaster doing?"

"Got turfed for borrowing money from the congregation to support his cocaine habit."

Damn, I miss our church!

PART V

🌱

How the Light Gets In

"There is a crack in everything,
That's how the light gets in."
Leonard Cohen, *Anthem*

Wedding Day

Dad and Luke

Channeling Björn

Dad conducts

Calvin and Luke

Dad and me

Raising Boys Right

Questionable motivations aside, going to church marked my beginnings as a writer. One day, Reverend Bob asked me to give a talk to the congregation about the challenge of raising boys. So, as an expert on the subject, I wrote a piece dealing with the issue of misogyny. I addressed the complacency among middle class parents regarding our own boys: that we needed to watch for signs of our sons objectifying women and to be vigilant regarding their vulnerability to peer and media influence.

The piece was called "Boys will be Boys – at whose and at what cost?"

The Sunday I delivered the talk, a woman in our congregation who wrote for the Toronto Star suggested I submit the written version to the Life Section. Well! Not only did the paper want to run it, but they offered to pay me one hundred and fifty bucks to do so! I was beyond thrilled. This marked the beginning of MY LIFE AS A WRITER. Not only that, the paper was going to send a photographer to take a picture of me with my fabulous, adoring, and, it goes without saying, well-behaved little boys. The editor suggested the guy come around four.

"Oh no, *Batman* is on at four. How about four thirty?"

The woman seemed somewhat taken aback, but agreed. She probably didn't have children, I thought.

I prepped the boys. Told their gooey, three and seven-year-old faces that this was the beginning of Mommy's writing career, and we were all going to have our pictures in the newspaper. Wasn't that exciting?

I took their flickering eyelids for interest, then added, "And if you're really good and hold still during the picture, I'll give you each a jumbo Oh Henry! chocolate bar. *Before* dinner!"

The next day, I plastered on make-up, did my hair and, just as Batman was wrapping up, peeked out my kitchen window to see the Star photographer waiting in his idling car. At 4:30, he was at the front door.

He wanted to get a shot of one of the kids offering me a cup of tea. They had never offered me tea in their short lives, but I was eager and ran to the cupboard to retrieve a blue and white Spode cup that would look great in the picture.

After quick introductions, the photographer said to three-year-old Calvin, "Ok young man, you sit next to your mom, and smile at her. And you," he said, proffering the cup to Luke, "you hand this to your Mom."

"No," said Luke.

I whipped out the two Oh Henry! bars, stashed strategically in the hip pockets of my jeans, and held them up like six shooters.

"Just a few moments, then you get these," I promised, in the saccharine singsong that I loathe in other mothers.

The boys focused like bird dogs on the bribes. Good.

Then I made a fatal mistake.

I picked up the remote and turned off the TV.

I might have pressed the nuclear launch button.

Calvin's face contorted in horror.

"POWER RANGERS! POWER RANGERS!" he shrieked.

Oh hell! I had strategized about Batman but forgotten what followed in the 4:30 slot.

Luke threw himself under the coffee table. Calvin dove in after him. Both boys, their faces red and contorted, screamed and writhed as I, the expert voice on child rearing for the Life Section of the Toronto Star, elbowed my way into the battle zone waving the Oh Henry! bars in their faces.

"Eat this, eat this!"

Suddenly, I was blinded by flashbulbs. The photographer had crouched down and was taking pictures of the three of us underneath the coffee table!

As I ducked a kick, I begged, "Don't shoot, don't shoot!"

Then, I saw his feet retreat and disappear. I wiggled from under the table and ran to the front window just in time to see his car speeding away from the curb.

Moments later, I was face down on my bed, sobbing. Calvin and Luke's worried little faces were six inches from my mine. They were crying too.

"Sorry Mommy, sorry Mommy."

I might have pulled myself together, if I thought I was traumatizing them, but their faces reeked of the Oh Henry! bars that they had managed to consume, before they came to see if I was killing myself.

I ramped up the guilt trip.

"Was it too much to ask? I will never have another chance like this in my life! I could have been a contender!" (Yes, I said that.)

Later that night, my friend from the Star called to see how it went. I told her.

She reassured me.

"I'll tell the editor it was a combat zone in there. She'll send someone else tomorrow."

The next day, the war photographer for the Toronto Star stood at my front door. His name was Boris. He was a huge Yugoslavian in a fur coat and a fur hat with the flaps tied up at the sides. A battered camera hung around his neck.

The boys, who had been told by their father that Christmas, Easter, birthdays, hockey and TV would be cancelled for the rest of their lives if they didn't behave, peeked at him from around the corner.

"Who are you?" boomed Boris.

"Luke."

"Calvin."

Their voices quavered. They had just met the giant.

"The other photographer thought we should get a shot of them serving me tea," I chirped.

"Eeez stupid idea," said Boris.

Then to the boys, "Vot games you like to play?"

"Batman," squeaked Luke, clutching his action figure of the Joker.

Calvin, holding tight to Batman, was too frightened to speak.

Boris pointed at me.

"You! Sit on sofa. And you guys, play with those – little guys."

The boys sat next to me then, complete with saliva-spraying vocal effects, staged a fight between Batman and the Joker.

"Now, look at your mother!" barked Boris.

Their heads snapped up, and two flashes fired off.

"All done," he announced.

I walked Boris to the door, and, as he put on his coat, I reached to hand him the camera that he had put on the hall table. It slipped. I caught it just in time.

"Phew! That was close."

"Don't worry. Eez tough," shrugged Boris. "This camera has seen Bosnia, Belfast, Vietnam. And now – has seen the Crawford boys."

The picture that accompanied the article the next day is one I will always treasure. Sure, the headline was "Boys will be Boys," but the image of my two sons looking up at me, their faces awash in fear-ridden obedience, proclaimed to the world – "She Raises Her Boys Right!"

Tell Jane...

In my mid-fifties, I flew to Calgary several times a year to visit my parents on their ranch southwest of the city. They were in their mid-eighties, and my dad in particular had worrying heart problems. Still, by all comparisons, he was doing better than well. He raked manure in the corrals, fed the horses and, after retiring from his sixty-year law practice, drove around the countryside to deliver meals on wheels to the "elderly."

On visits home, I would go with him on these junkets. We'd had an ongoing disagreement about whether or not he should drive. Dad behind the wheel was a heart stopping experience. He had undiagnosed glaucoma and had lost all peripheral vision. This caused him to zig-zag all over the highway, as we puttered along in search of the "shut-ins." One day, to my enormous relief, he allowed me to drive. But when we got to the first destination, I made the mistake of leaping out of the car to retrieve the meal from the trunk. I didn't want his arthritic body to have to lean over, much less carry the large tray up the flagstone path.

But as I reached into the trunk, he barked irascibly, "Now never mind, I'm doing that!"

I looked at his him and knew that his concession about the driving was as far as he was ready to go; that every bit of independence he relinquished was, for him, a step closer to death. So I stood back and watched as he lifted out the tray, as he concentrated on overcoming his pain. Then, I followed him, my arms spread wide, ready to make a save, as he listed back and forth up the path to deliver the meal to the spry, seventy-year-old woman waiting inside.

At the end of this visit, when I hugged Dad goodbye, I was careful not to hold him too tight, as I felt the frailty of his body, and the pain he silently endured. Not until my plane took off and circled east away from the foothills did I put on my dark glasses and let the tears spill. Was this goodbye our last? It hit me then that it wasn't so much the losing him that filled me with sorrow. He had led a rich, eventful life. My deep ache came from this realization: that I had never told my father how much I loved him, nor the many ways of why.

Never had my dad said he loved me. Such declarations were considered gooey, over the top, suspect even. Was it a generational thing – that giving words to deep feelings trivialized them? Suddenly, I realized that the thought of telling Dad I loved him made me anxious.

When I got home, I took the issue to my therapist.

"What do you think is going to happen?" she asked.

"Shock, suspicion. An 'oh Eve!' that he always says, whenever I get intense, emotional or theatrical about anything."

My therapist and I role-played scenarios.

I would practice saying, "Dad, I love you."

She threw back every possible negative reaction then counseled me to hold up my hand when "he" objected, and say, "I just wanted you to know. It might not be important to you, but it is important to me to tell you this."

If necessary, I was to leave the room to give him time to digest this offensive declaration.

On my next trip, I decided it would be best to get this mission over with, so I could relax for the rest of my visit. The time to do it would be over pre-dinner drinks. I rarely drink, but on this visit, that was a non-negotiable. I chose gin – otherwise known as Valium on ice.

But the gin didn't work. Every night, as we sat chatting and sipping, I looked for an opening to segue into the subject of love. But by the time I got up the courage to take the plunge, my parents had started their nightly fight about who knew best how to cook the frozen peas. I would step into the role of umpire, knowing that the only solution was to get them both fed.

After dinner, I'd shoosh them off to bed over their protestations that they wanted to help clean up. Fifteen minutes later, Dad would enter the kitchen in his knee-length nightshirt, his skinny legs and bare feet completing the picture. He'd pour his milk, take his pills, then retreat, tossing a "goodnight dear" over his shoulder.

Another chance gone.

The last night of my visit, I was desperate. I could barely hear what Mom and Dad were talking about. As their mouths moved up and down, the voice in my head yammered, *say it, say it!* When I heard the word "peas," I panicked.

I slammed down my gin, and said, "You know what Dad?"

I took a big breath. Big mistake. In that second, Dad interjected.

"Oh Eve! Do you know what that friend of yours, Jane, said to me the other day?"

Jane had been a close friend since childhood. Her parents were my parents' best friends. She had a deeply developed spiritual practice, was down to earth and had a throw your head back, roaring laugh. I loved Jane.

"What, Dad?" I asked, derailed.

"We were at the Country Club for dinner, and she turns to me and says, 'George, do you ever tell your girls, that you love them?'"

"What did you tell her?"

"I told her I'd never heard anything so ridiculous in my life! All that meditation stuff has made her go nutso. I said, 'No, Jane, I don't have to tell them. They know I love them by the things I *do*. By my actions.'"

I nodded feebly.

"Still, Dad, it might be nice to hear it out loud sometime."

He stared at me, as if I had just said something rude. Then he stood up.

"Ok! Let's get those peas on."

Alone in the kitchen after dinner, I was in despair. I had thought my difficulty declaring my feelings was of my own making. But my instincts were right on. Declarations of love *were* met with ridicule, labeled "nutso" and over the top.

As I dried the last pot, Dad shuffled in to swallow down his milk and pills. He looked at the gleaming kitchen.

"Thank you, dear. We're going to miss you, when you go tomorrow."

I gave him a careful hug.

"Night Dad."

He gave me a peck on the cheek.

"Good night, dear."

Then, as his nightshirt and skinny legs shuffled out of the kitchen, I heard him say over his shoulder, "Tell Jane I love you."

The Listening Heart

When my son was eight years old, he told me he was gay. And then I changed his mind.

It happened after dinner. I was lying on my bed reading, when, suddenly, I was aware of Calvin standing in the doorway.

"Mom?"

"Yes."

He flew across the room, landing face-down next to me on the king-size bed. He buried his large, curly-topped head into the pillow. His body was rigid, his voice muffled.

"I think I'm gay."

The moment that followed could only be described as a vacuum, a nothingness, a big – empty. Then, in flooded a wave of terror beyond reason, or personal belief, or conditioning. I was an actor. I had close friends who were gay! In the eighties, at the height of the AIDS epidemic, and while pregnant with my first son, I had helped care for one of them as he battled, unsuccessfully, with the disease. My first son bears that man's name.

I put my hand on the back of Calvin's head. His curls were damp with fear.

"What makes you think that?"

I wondered at the calm in my voice.

"Luke told me."

I exhaled. His twelve-year-old brother had been going through a phase, along with his peers, where he called everything gay. *You're so gay, this dinner's gay, that chair is gay.* I should have stopped him, told him how derogatory it was, but, to be honest, I was so exhausted putting out other fires, I had become deaf to anything but the loudest sirens. A few months earlier, my husband and I had separated, and my two boys and I were navigating the turbulent seas of our new reality.

I wrapped my arms around Calvin and kissed the top of his head. I pointed to the laundry hamper sitting in the middle of the bedroom floor.

"Calvin, look at the laundry basket over there. What colour is it?"

"Blue," he snuffled.

"Right. Now, if Luke called it red, would that make it red?"

"No."

"So, why would him calling you gay, make you gay?"

I felt his body relax a bit. And as his body relaxed, so did mine.

"Now, let's go run a bath, and then we'll wade through some more Harry Potter."

To this day, I cannot look back on that conversation without pain and deep shame. My beloved little boy had put his trust in me, and I didn't listen. Oh, I heard him all right. But I couldn't handle it. And instead of staying with him and acknowledging that what his body told me was true, I put my fears ahead of his and dismissed his eight-year-old courage. And with this dismissal, I signaled to him that what he told me was not acceptable. I betrayed his trust, leaving him to carry this burden of shame, my shame, for another seven years.

When he was fifteen, he told me again.

We were at the family ranch outside Calgary. My niece was getting married the next day, and Calvin and I had come for the wedding. I was to MC the reception, and that evening, with the help of my sister, Marti, I was trying to decide on an outfit that would be sexy but tasteful.

The atmosphere at the ranch had been subdued. My father had died in March. A month later, my oldest sister, Sharon, was diagnosed with terminal cancer and would die within the year.

Added to that, my relationship with Calvin was strained. Over New Years, we had had a major blowout following a drinking incident that had his father and me at his bedside in the emergency ward at Sunnybrook Hospital in Toronto. Once he recovered, I set limits that he refused to honour. So, when he told me he wanted to go live with his dad, I said, "Go ahead." The next day, he told me he'd changed his mind. I thought of all the books and experts that say stick with it! If you back down, he'll never respect you. Against all instincts, I packed his things and stood there. He stormed out. I thought he'd be back in a week. He didn't come home for a year.

I cried a lot, I went to parenting groups, I read books on raising teens, I went to counseling with him, where, as the therapist looked on in silence, Calvin stood over me and spat, "I hate you. I hate you. You're, you're always – there!"

He told me I had to stop calling him sweetheart. In the days after the divorce, why, he asked, had I always rescued him from weekends at his dad's when he called me begging to come home? How was I supposed to *learn* anything if I did that? I had to stop talking about him to my friends. I had to stop babying him.

But I could still do his laundry.

161

When I drove him to his tennis clinics, he'd stare out the window in sullen silence. When he did talk, he compared me, unfavourably, to his dad, and then slammed the door when I dropped him off.

A week before he died, my ninety-year-old father called to ask how things were going.

"You have to let him know you love him," said Dad.

"I do! I have!"

"Yes, but he thinks you kicked him out."

"I didn't!"

"But he *thinks* you did. Just let him know you love him."

As I hung up, I felt my heart constrict. Had I thrown him out?

The phone rang again. It was Dad.

"Dear, I don't want you to think I was criticizing you."

"Don't worry Dad. It's good to hear what you think."

I told him I loved him then hung up. It was the last conversation we ever had.

By summer, tensions were easing a bit, and though Calvin was still living with his father, he accepted my invitation to go to Vancouver, then, on the way back to Toronto, stop over in Calgary for the wedding. Aside from some moody episodes, things had gone pretty well. So, on that early August evening at the ranch, as my sister and I focused on our dress choices, I didn't think anything of it when he came into the bedroom.

"Mom, can we go for a walk?"

A note in his voice put me on alert. His body, now taller than mine, was seized with terror, and, once again, my physical response matched his. I dropped the dress I was holding on the bed.

162

"Yes, let's go now."

Once outside, we walked in silence to the gate that separated the house from the rest of the ranch. By the time we were halfway down the field, he started to shake. His face contorted, as he fought back tears. A nauseating dread washed through me. Had he hurt someone, stolen something, have a drug addiction?

"I love you," he said.

"I love you too."

"I have to say it."

"It doesn't matter what you have to say Calvin. I love you."

"I'm gay."

Then, this 6' 2" athletic honours student collapsed in my arms and sobbed. He was drenched in sweat, all muscles seized.

His not-yet-mature voice broke through the sobs, as he croaked, "I'm so sorry, Mom. I'll never be able to give you grandchildren."

I tightened my arms around him, and told him over and over that I loved him, that everything was going to be ok. Then, I guided him back to the house and told him to get in the car. I called in to my mom and sister that Calvin and I were going for a drive to look for deer – a tradition we had shared with his brother since we first started coming for our summer visits.

The evening was golden, the shadows long, and the air sweet with the scent of fresh-cut hay. As I drove down the gravel road, my heart was pounding, my mouth dry, as instructions from "parenthood" sessions echoed in my head. *Stay calm!* But I was not calm. I was terror-stricken and, at the same time, bewildered by the feeling. Some of my best friends were – but *my* boy? No.

We drove to the vacant tennis courts close to the hamlet near the ranch. Our love of tennis had been the one connecting thread that had held us together over the past painful year. As we sat in the car, looking through the fence at the courts, a calm descended. This was our church, our sanctuary. Calvin's breathing started to even, as he unloaded his heart.

I look back on it now, and still can't make sense of the fear that roiled through me. Oddly, my very first thought when he said, "I'm gay," was – *you'll never be able to go to Iran.*

Was that a distillation of the prejudice and danger I knew he might face? Perhaps. But something more selfish was at play. I had plans for this kid. Since his birth, I had relished his company, his imagination, his fierce intelligence, his athleticism. Most of all, I relished our connection. I had envisioned the woman he might marry, the children he would have. I had projected *my* view of life on *his* life and, suddenly, that construct had come toppling down in three words. I am gay. We don't have it in our family, I thought, and with that thought, bubbled up a deeply buried belief, that homosexuality was an affliction. If not, why had it only recently been legalized, why the need for secrecy, the language around it: in the closet, coming out, he's that way? Poofter, queer, fairy, faggot – all less than.

As we sat at the tennis courts, I asked him how he knew. He said he didn't know.

And then – I did it again. I gave him an out. I gave *me* an out.

I heard myself say, "Maybe you don't have to know. At your

age, there's confusion about all sorts of things. It's as if you're driving through a fog, scared you can't see. But you don't have to see that far. You only have go as far as your headlights allow. Then you creep along, until you can see a bit more."

But I was the one in the fog; I was the one who needed to take it as far as the headlights.

Calvin left for Toronto the day after the wedding. I stayed on for an extended visit with my mother and sister. Though Calvin had sworn me to secrecy, I was bursting with confusion, loneliness and pain. One day, over lunch with my sister at a Calgary restaurant, I blurted out Calvin's confession then burst into tears. I don't know what I expected her reaction to be, but her words, her tone of voice, were a soothing balm.

"I think that's wonderful."

As I snuffled into my napkin, she went on.

"I have a strong feeling about people who are gay. They bring a sensibility to the world, they enrich us. We need them."

"But – I just can't picture him having sex," I blurted.

"Oh for God's sake! Who pictures anyone having sex? It's disgusting."

I let out a whoop, then the two of us dissolved. We held our napkins to our faces to hide from the irritated looks of nearby diners.

Laughter – the tonic of the gods.

Shortly after my return to Toronto, Calvin came back from his dad's to live with me.

One evening, he said, "Mom, remember what I told you at the ranch? I don't think I am."

"Oh, ok," I said too quickly.

He started to date and had "sort of" girlfriends. He competed

165

in tennis tournaments, complete with packs of gorgeous babes cheering him on. He excelled at school. All was well. Denial, in full force, gave us a reprieve.

The summer before his final year of high school, Calvin, along with a friend, went to Paris with Calvin's dad. When he got back, Calvin was not speaking to his father. Apparently, over dinner at a restaurant, his dad had made homophobic jokes, flapping his wrist and talking about queers.

I told my friend Marie about this. Marie-Helene, my close friend and confidant, was Calvin's own, personal "Auntie Mame." She first met him when he was five, and it was love at first sight for both of them. That he confided in her over the years never troubled me. I was a great believer in "it takes a village to raise a child."

As I was in mid-diatribe about my ex-husband's anti-gay prejudice, Marie interrupted me.

"Are you listening! This is not about his father. He phoned me yesterday. He is going to tell you."

"Oh," I said.

The next day, as we sat at a pub near the tennis courts, Calvin, for the third time in his life, said, "Mom, I am gay."

And yes, at last, I listened.

"Oh are you? That's ok."

It would be a sweet ending to suggest that all went smoothly from that point on, but the following year was a turbulent one. Calvin made individual appointments with each of his friends to come out to them, and then swore them to secrecy, until he could tell the next one.

I suggested that once one knew, they all knew.

"My friends don't break promises," he shot back.

It was intense, it was tiring. His anger toward me continued in intermittent bursts. He accused me of treating him like a baby, always nagging and reminding him of things. I vowed to do better, so, when I saw him head out the door to a tennis match with no water bottle, I pressed my lips together in silence. An hour later, as I watched courtside, he came to the fence and beckoned me over. Wiping his red, sweaty face on a towel, he said, "Could you go get me a ginormous Gatorade?"

"No."

"Why not?"

"You told me not to baby you."

He was aghast.

"I'll tell you when to baby me and when not to!"

One evening, as I sat at the kitchen table, Calvin was hurling a verbal barrage of teenage angst at me. At this point, his older brother, Luke, poked his head through the doorway. He had just come in from skateboarding. His cheeks were rosy, his "No Rules" t-shirt soaked in sweat.

"What's going on?"

"None of your business!" snapped Calvin.

"Well – you're yelling at *her*."

Her was Luke's new name for me. He had started calling me Eve when he turned thirteen. A few years later, in the middle of a fight, I blurted that he was to stop calling me Eve, that I hated it. I am your mother! To his credit, he did stop, but he couldn't quite make the leap to Mom, and so, when he needed my attention, he called me she, her or hey!

Calvin whirled on Luke.

"Why don't you call me a faggot, Luke! That's what you've

167

done my whole life."

"No I haven't."

"Yes you have! For years you've said, 'You're so gay, Calvin. You're so gay.'"

Luke slumped against the doorframe.

"Yeah, well, *everything* is gay. I call *her* gay, that chair gay, the colour of this kitchen is really gay. Are you?"

"Yes, I am! I am gay!"

Luke shrugged.

"Well – I don't care."

Then, he turned to leave the room.

"Where are you going? I'm not finished!" cried Calvin.

"Well I am. You're starting to repeat yourself, so I'm done here."

Then he left. Calvin and I looked after him, united in our slack-jawed amazement.

Was life that simple?

By springtime of his final year, Calvin had pretty much informed the world of his sexual identity. He started looking into US tennis scholarships, and, on a phone call with the coach from the University of Tennessee, I heard him say to the woman, "I have one thing to run by you. I'm not sure if this matters – but I'm gay."

He listened for a moment, then said, "Oh, ok. That's fine." Then, he hung up.

"What did she say?" I asked.

"She said, 'We don't have much of that down here.'"

I wanted to spring through the phone and throttle the woman.

Shortly after, Calvin made the decision to forget about tennis and decided to go to McGill University in Montreal, where he spent four blessed years in one of the best, most diverse and accepting universities in the country.

In April, I booked two rooms for us in Montreal and arranged a road trip to go check out the place. A few days before we were to leave, he told me he didn't want to go. I encouraged him to bring his long-time friend, Jacob; that it would be fun. A day later, he told me that Jacob couldn't come, but his friend, Eliot, could. I had recently met Eliot. Eliot wasn't just gay. He was cartoon gay. And now, these two seventeen-year-old boys were to share a hotel room next to mine? Would I allow Luke to share with a girl – should he ever find one – at that age? No! And I told Calvin so.

"Oh, so now you're homophobic!"

I wanted to bark, don't you dare play the gay card with me. This is about what's appropriate at seventeen. I wouldn't let Luke do it!

But I was struck dumb. I had been completely manipulated.

That night, I called a close friend for guidance.

"This is April," she said. "By September, he will be out of your clutches and doing whatever the hell he wants."

So, I relented and, a couple of days later, found myself checking into a Montreal hotel with the two boys.

At the front desk, I said to Calvin, "Before you two go to your room, I want you to go to the convenience store and buy me a six-pack of beer. Nothing under 5% alcohol, though if you find something stronger, that would be better.

I am going to have a nap, then I want the two of you in my

room at six to go for dinner."

A half hour later, I was sitting cross-legged on the bed in my hotel room sipping beer from a plastic glass and trying not to think of the two boys in the adjoining room.

It was then that a strange thing happened. I had a sensation I can only describe as otherworldly.

I am not particularly religious, but Christ's words, "Come unto me, all ye that labour and are heavy laden, and I will give you rest," whispered like a gentle breeze through my being. At the same time, I felt as though a massive weight was being lifted from my shoulders, and, following that, came a profound sense of peace. I lay back on the bed and fell into a deep sleep.

An hour later, the two boys joined me for a beer, then the three of us walked down to Old Montreal, where we had dinner on the outdoor terrace of an Italian restaurant. The evening was soft and unusually warm for April. Above the shops across the street, people sat on Juliet balconies, their legs dangling through the railings. As I watched them, sipping wine and chatting, one woman caught my eye and waved. The "Frenchness" of old Montreal was sheer bliss. Calvin, Eliot and I shared stories and laughter then, afterwards, wandered the streets looking for the perfect ice cream cone.

Later, we parted ways on St. Catherine Street. The boys were off on a pub-crawl. I told them I would see them in the morning.

As I watched them walk off down the street, I felt my heart, at last – surrender. And with that release, came the tears. But this time, they were tears of warmth and of light. They were tears of love.

Was it that simple?

As an actor, I knew that simple wasn't easy. It's often a long, hard journey to get to simple.

Well… except maybe for Luke.

I wiped my eyes and smiled. Then, I turned down the street to the hotel.

PART VI

I Paint Gophers!

Mom's gopher for Wayne

I Paint Gophers!

The phone woke me. It was my sister, Marti, calling me from the Foothillls Hospital in Calgary.

"Mom's hallucinating. She's sinking in and out of consciousness."

I sat up and clutched the pillow to my chest.

Our mother, at ninety-two, had had an ongoing stomach bleed for two years that defied medical treatment. The only thing that kept her alive was weekly blood transfusions. Every week, one of my sisters took her to the hospital, where, for a period of three hours, she received the slow drip of life that raised her blood count, only to bleed out as the week progressed, when she would lapse again into a sleepy, life-threatening anemia.

Marti continued.

"She's slipping into a coma."

I took a deep breath to ease the growing knot in my stomach.

"I'll get the first flight I can."

Then, an afterthought.

"Marti, has she had a bowel movement recently? Didn't a nurse tell us that, with this bleed, if she doesn't have proper bowel movements, there could be a build-up of toxins that cause hallucinations?"

Full disclosure. Bowel movements happen to be my particular area of expertise. I lay this obsession directly at my mother's feet.

As a child, if I was sick, her first question was, "Have you done a 'Big Job?'"

If I hesitated, she marched to the bathroom cupboard then chased after me with a hose and enema bag! Once she had administered the cure, she gave me a "Dennis the Menace" comic book to read, to distract me from relieving myself too soon.

Years later, my two young boys and I were visiting Mom and Dad at their ranch south of Calgary. Our nanny, Gail, had come with us to give me time alone with my parents and, for that matter, myself. Gail, a Jamaican woman with an outstanding operatic voice, was a true friend. We shared a lot of laughs and tag-teamed effortlessly with the kids. Our conversation regularly centered on the state of our bowels. Gail had a particularly rough time with hers. So it was no surprise that, when we all piled into the car with Mom to go on an outing, Gail whispered to me that she was painfully constipated.

"We'll stop at the general store and get some Ex-lax," I reassured her.

As we neared our front gate, I leaned from my position in the back seat and said, "Mom, Gail's constipated, so I thought we would –"

Mom slammed on the brakes, bringing the car to a shuddering halt on the cattle guard. She turned to Gail who sat next to her in the front seat.

"We'll take you straight to emerg!" she said, doing her best to stay calm.

"No, Mom! We just need to get her some Ex-lax."

Mom eyed Gail suspiciously. "Are you sure?"

The next morning, Gail intercepted me on my way to the kitchen.

"Any results?" I asked, eagerly.

"Results! I was up all night. I didn't think two squares would be enough, so, I ate the whole –"

"You didn't!" I said.

An hour later, Gail was out in the driveway, watching the boys as they rode their trikes and shot hoops. She was singing a soaring aria from Madame Butterfly. I was at the kitchen table with Mom. Her glasses were perched on the end of her nose, as she worked her crossword. But, as Gail's lyric soprano floated in the morning air, she put down her puzzle, took off her glasses and looked heavenward.

Utterly transported, she sighed, "I wish I could sing like that after a bowel movement."

Later that afternoon, as the plane lifted off, I was too anxious to read or watch a movie. My thoughts drifted back to a morning two years earlier, when I had received a similar phone call from Marti. That one had me airborne to San Francisco. Only this time, it was for Dad.

He and Mom had decided to go on a two-week cruise. Marti and I had been frantic about this decision. At ninety, Dad had been experiencing recurring dizzy spells and some falls. We insisted he get clearance from his doctor to travel.

The doc had told Dad, with a macho slap, "Of course you're good to go. Just don't get eaten by a shark."

At my father's funeral, this same man said to me, "Well your Dad had such advanced coronary disease, it was bound to happen."

Did he not consider what it would be like for my mother to have Dad die in San Francisco, or worse, on the cruise ship? Did he not consider that Dad was hoping he would say, no, you can't go? That he lived in constant pain and was simply worn out? That he was making this trip for Mom?

Marti flew to San Francisco with Mom and Dad, to make sure they got on the ship. But upon arrival, Dad fell ill. He couldn't pee. At the hospital, the doctor told him he was in renal failure, catheterized him to give him relief and urged him to go home to Calgary the next day.

That evening, Mom and Marti got Dad back to the hotel then ordered room service. Mom, in her anxiety, nagged Dad to drink water. Marti later told me that he kept stroking his ear and had a distant look on his face – as though he was listening to someone else.

She asked, "Dad, would you drink some water if I put some Scotch in it?"

"Oh yes dear, that would be good."

Minutes later, Marti and Mom decided to retreat to Marti's room to give Dad some quiet, in the hope that he'd fall asleep.

As she tucked him into bed, Mom said, "I'm sorry I was so mean to you about the water."

"That's ok," he said. "You were just fussing."

Words of forgiveness and comfort – the last words he would speak.

Later, when Marti walked Mom back to her room, they found Dad lifeless. Marti, in a panic, called the desk. It was a decision she would later regret.

"I knew he was gone, Eve. He wasn't – in the room."

They were staying at the prestigious Mark Hopkins hotel, and, in an instant, nine paramedics were in the room. They threw Dad on the floor, pounded and shocked his frail chest, until a pulse came back, then rushed him to hospital, where drugs were administered to bring back blood pressure. He was technically alive but in a coma.

When I got the call from Marti on that early morning in March, she told me that our two sisters, Sharon and Suzie, were already on their way.

"I will get there as fast as I can," I told her. "I need to talk to him, Marti. People can hear even in comas. The last thing that goes is hearing, right?"

"Eve, he's gone. He's left his body. He's not here anymore."

But I couldn't listen. I had to talk to him. Tell him one last time – how much I loved him.

At the airport, a suspicious customs officer asked me why I had a one-way ticket.

"My father is in a coma. I don't know if I will be coming back to Toronto or going to Calgary for a funeral."

"I am sorry," she said, gently, as she returned my passport.

I had held it together until then. But her kind response did me in. I walked over to a nearby wall, slid down to the floor, cupped my hands over my eyes and sobbed.

Six hours later, I arrived at the hotel and dragged my bag onto the elevator then down a long hallway.

Mom opened the door. My three sisters were sitting on the bed. I fell into Mom's arms. She hugged me tight.

"How is he? Can I go see him?"

I didn't hear her muffled reply. Confused, I pulled back.

"Mom, is he alive?"

"No."

"But, I need to talk to him!"

"Eve, he was gone. He wouldn't have heard you."

She wrapped her arms around me as I wept on her shoulder. A few seconds later, she gently pushed me back and brushed a curl from my forehead. She studied me for a moment, and then, I saw a flicker of disapproval cross her face.

"You've grown your hair."

"I wanted a change," I snuffled defensively.

Sharon blew her nose into a piece of toilet paper.

"Mom, are you saying she's too *old* for long hair?"

Mom sat me on the bed, handed me the roll of toilet paper, and then settled next to me. She held my hand as my tears continued to spill. A minute or so later, she eyed my unruly mop again.

"What will you do with it for the funeral?"

"Pin it up," I blubbered.

"Oh good. I like up-dos."

I looked out the plane's window at the patchwork quilt of the prairies below and felt myself smile at the memory. When I turned back, I saw a frail, elderly woman move slowly down the aisle to the washroom. Did Mom look like that to others? Not to me. As weak as she had become, all I ever saw was her core. And it was valiant, warrior-like.

A month after Dad's funeral, Mom had been diagnosed with a virulent cancer of the parotid gland. Surgery was followed by six weeks of radiation that left her face burned and swathed in bandages. During this time, Marti and I helped her move from the ranch into a senior's home in Calgary. It was called The Fountains. No "of youth" at the end.

As she recovered and settled in to her new home, she oddly became more relaxed and happy. The stress of worrying about Dad had lifted. She reunited with many long-time friends at The Fountains, women she had known during the war and our growing up years in Calgary.

Another sign that Mom had embraced her new life was when she set up an easel in the living room of her small apartment. She had taken up painting twenty years earlier – with mixed results. But it engaged her for hours on end and was something she could call her own.

A few years earlier, while visiting my parents, I discovered a canvas tucked away behind the freezer. It was an oil painting of a large gopher standing up on its hind legs against the backdrop of the Rocky Mountains. The gopher was massive in comparison to the Rockies. It looked as if Godzilla had landed – a frightening vision, but for the beatific smile on the gopher's face and a smudge above its head, where Mom, in her attempt to blend some paint, had inadvertently created a halo. Godzilla or the Second Coming? In the foreground, there was a small, rat-like figure peering out from behind a boulder. It gazed up at this mother of all gophers. This little mutant was meant to be the gopher's baby. Obviously, Big Mama had stood too near a microwave during her confinement.

I started to laugh. No, I started to squeal. Mom rounded the corner from the kitchen to find me clutching the large canvas to my chest.

"You weren't supposed to see that!"

"What were you thinking?"

"I was working on perspective," she said defensively.

It occurred to me that tactless was too kind a word to describe my behaviour, so I held my breath and said, "Actually, the gopher has a very sweet face, and the tree looks good."

"Oh, too late, too late," Mom said crossly. "If it makes you laugh so much, Eve, you can keep it."

Then she stomped back to the kitchen.

That was how I became the proud owner of Mom's first – in a series! – of gopher paintings. When I got home, I had it framed and hung it in my living room, where it took pride of place among the works of renowned Western artists.

One particular fan of Mom's gopher painting was my friend, Wayne. Wayne is not just a psychiatrist; he's a Renaissance man. Among his many areas of interest is art. Whenever he came for dinner, Wayne would look at the Godzilla gopher and laugh, not in a derisive way, but from pure delight.

Now, if telling Mom that I had hung the gopher in my living room mollified her, telling her that Wayne loved it left her ecstatic, which is why, while recovering from radiation, she decided to paint a gopher for his 75th birthday. Again, perspective was a challenge, but the same could be said of Picasso, right? This particular gopher stood on its hind legs under a massive sunflower that had dropped a single, yellow petal that balanced like a spike on the end of its nose. The gopher, in its attempt to examine this petal, had turned cross-eyed.

But, the most fascinating aspect of the work was the gopher's tail. Gophers have short, stubby tails. This gopher had a massive, long tail that extended between its legs, effectively holding it up. I viewed the painting propped on the counter to dry.

"Mom, what is that large, phallicy thing poking out between the gopher's legs?"

Mom, her face swathed in white bandages, adjusted her glasses and took a look.

"Oh. Oh dear."

Then she started to laugh, as much as the pain from her radiated face would allow. But she didn't change it. She simply wrote a message on the back.

"Dear Wayne, Happy Birthday! I hope you remain as curious as this gopher! Sheila."

Wayne hung it in his office. It is positioned next to a Gauguin print and seems to have become the new Rorschach test for his patients. He tells me they rarely fail to comment.

Mom went on to paint a third gopher for a friend of mine in Calgary who was struggling with prostate cancer. She wanted to cheer him up. Sadly, he died before she finished, but his brother, who was also Mom's lawyer, asked if he could have it. I have never seen it. Marti says I don't want to. It now hangs in this man's law office.

The sound of the landing gears brought me back to the present moment and with it a chest-tightening dread. Please let her be alive. I had to tell her how much I loved her. I could not miss being with her, the way I had missed being with Dad.

At the hospital, I scanned for her room number as I hurried down the hall. I found it, took a deep breath and walked in.

There she was, sitting up in bed, watching TV, three I.V.'s running into the ropy veins of her bruised hand.

"Mom! You're ok!"

"Yes!" she exclaimed, with delight. "Turns out, all I needed was a good enema! Isn't that always the way?"

Moments later, Marti rounded the corner with a cup of coffee.

"You were right, Eve. Toxins in the bowels."

I did a victory fist pump, then the two of us settled in to chat with Mom. When she drifted off, Marti beckoned me out to the hall.

"A doctor from palliative care is coming round. The docs think, because she's not getting any better, they should stop transfusing her."

"You mean kill her? She's fine! They just don't want her using up the blood supply. What did you say?"

"I just cried. They said parents sometimes cling to life because they sense the kids aren't ready to let them go. They think someone should talk to Mom, while she still has her wits about her. Let her make up her own mind."

"Do you think she wants to go, Marti?"

"I don't know. She's hard to read. Anyway, how do we ask her? Hey Mom, you ready to die yet?"

When Mom woke, Marti and I pulled chairs up to her bedside. The three of us watched a CNN report about a worldwide rice shortage. News footage showed hoarders at Costco carting away large sacks of rice.

Moments later, an elegant woman in a white lab coat entered the room. She checked the thick file she was carrying.

"Mrs. Crawford? I am Dr. Burns from palliative care. I wonder if I could talk to you for a few minutes."

She spoke in the velvet tones of the woman on Air Canada

who tells you how to put on your life preserver. Marti and I dutifully moved away and perched on the windowsill.

Dr. Burns pulled up a chair next to Mom and said, "First, Mrs. Crawford, could I please ask you to spell the word 'world' backwards?"

This was the *do you have your wits about you?* test.

"D L R O W."

Mom just rattled it off!

I was astonished. Witless me had run aground at L.

Even Dr. Burns seemed impressed.

"Very good."

Mom smiled proudly. She was minus her front dentures and looked like a seven-year-old who had just won the spelling bee.

Then, Dr. Burns got down to business.

"Now, Mrs. Crawford, you have been through some pretty rough times."

"Oh, not that bad."

"You must be getting pretty weary of these weekly trips to hospital for transfusions."

"Oh no," enthused Mom. "The people in the transfusion unit are wonderful. We've become great friends."

Dr. Burns looked confused. Her agenda was taking a hit.

"Well, that's lovely. Still, we want to let you know that if you get tired of these endless trips to hospital, these constant transfusions, you only have to say, 'Enough! No more!' and we will stop them. And we promise to keep you perfectly comfortable."

Suddenly, Mom realized that this was no friendly chat. Her face transformed into a Charlie Brown cartoon, as her lips pressed together in a flat line.

"I don't want to stop the transfusions," she said, evenly.

Then, she crossed her arms, leveled a look at Dr. Burns, and proclaimed, "I PAINT GOPHERS!"

Dr. Burns cast a knowing look towards Marti and me, that said, "Hallucinating."

She turned back to Mom.

"Well that's – lovely."

"No!" I said. "She does! She actually does paint gophers."

But Mom didn't need back up. She was on a roll.

"I also paint penguins and polar bears!"

Then, at full throttle, she started to sing!

"'I'm going to keep right on to the end of the road!' Do you know that song?"

Dr. Burns' Air Canada voice went up a notch.

"No. Maybe. I'm not sure."

"Well, *I* am going to keep right on and around the bend!"

Then, she gave Dr. Burns a dismissive wave, looked at the TV, and declared, "They've got to start planting potatoes."

"Her solution to the rice shortage!" I called after the doctor, who was in full retreat.

Mom lived for two more years. During that time, she grew progressively weaker. We transferred her to a long-term care facility, where she moved from cane, to walker, to wheelchair. What amazed us was her serene acceptance of each setback. As her physical world became more confined, she used her remaining energy to fuel her curiosity about this life. During my frequent visits, the two of us tried to figure out the difference between a Shiite and a Sunni. Mom explained to me the meaning of counter-insurgency. I asked if she believed in an afterlife. Her answer? "Energy can neither be created nor destroyed." She told me that every night, as she lay in bed looking at the tall pine tree outside her window, she knew there must be a god.

On fall days, I wheeled her along the pathway skirting the Glenmore dam. We found a bench where I could sit, and together, in silence, we'd look at the Rockies, blue in the distance, and listen to the rattle of the drying leaves. As a young mother of four girls, Mom used to ride her horse along this path in what was country then.

Marti and I, in an effort to find something more exciting for her to drink than Ensure, had established a ritual during each visit of bringing her a Starbucks hot chocolate, topped with whipped cream. Each and every time she drank it, she would close her eyes and pronounce euphorically, "This is the best thing I have ever had in my life!"

In what was to be the last weeks of her life, Mom didn't have the energy to converse, so I read to her. She loved the stories of James Herriot, especially "All Creatures Great and Small." It was about a veterinarian in a small Yorkshire town and reflected her lifetime enchantment with nature and animals.

One day, she was having trouble hearing, so I lay down next to her and read into her ear. Squeezing into the single hospital bed with its raised bars was no easy feat. She was unable to move from her prone position without the help of three assistants, and her repeated feedings of hot chocolate had turned her into a solid citizen, so there was no way I could shift her over. This meant that I had to lie on my side, one hand propping up my head, the other holding the book. That day, as

187

I got into the story, I realized it was about the death of an Irish setter.

"Is this too sad for you Mom?"

"No."

I read on. Soon, my neck started to spasm, and my rotator cuff threatened to tear. Flipping pages was acrobatic. At last, Mom closed her eyes and drifted off. I closed the book and carefully started to extricate myself from her bed. Just as I felt the welcome rush of blood into my joints, her eyes popped open.

"Why have you stopped?"

"Would you like me to read more?"

"Yes please."

So, I kept going, willing the discomfort away. At the same time, I reveled in the feeling of my body lying alongside my mother's – of the growing warmth between us. I don't know if we made it through to the dog's death, but I do know that in reading to my mother that day, I had an epiphany.

On the way out of the building, as I passed the elderly parked in wheelchairs in front of the big screen TV, as I passed the demented wandering the halls with frightened faces, and the caregivers trying to spoon slop into disinterested mouths, it struck me how deprived old people are of physical contact. How often does someone massage their neck or feet? Or hug them long enough for that embrace to linger in their body memory?

Mom died two weeks later. And, as it was with Dad, I was in flight and missed her passing. When I got to the hospital, Suzie and Marti were still at her side. They told me she had been sleeping in peace, and that the two of them started talking about the many horses she had had throughout her life. So as not to wake her, they quietly named them: Patsy, Dandy, Rosie, Kitty, Rodney, Bobby. When they looked up, she was gone.

I kissed her cooling forehead and wept. I hadn't made it. But solace came in knowing that the last memory she had of me was of a warm body lying next to hers, and a gentle story whispered in her ear.

Acknowledgements

My sincere thanks to Rosemary Dunsmore for first suggesting that I turn my stories into a book.

My gratitude goes to Frances Itani. I treasure our years of friendship and shared laughter, and I thank you for your generous guidance on the craft of writing.

To Richard Ouzounian and the Ouzounian family (Pam, Kat and Michael) for the countless gourmet meals you have served me over our forty (ouch!) years of friendship. It has been at your table that many of my stories found their first audience. I owe you a gazillion dinners and promise that once I move beyond my recipe for frozen peas, the invitation is in the mail.

Thanks to Sarah O'Sullivan for proofing *Gophers*, and a special thanks to Aaron Rachel Brown for formatting *Gophers* and for your wonderful, wacky cover design.

Finally, I want to thank Heidi von Palleske of Smart House Books who has made *I Paint Gophers!* a reality. Heidi is passion and compassion all in one package. Plus, she's really, really smart.

I Paint Gophers! is about family and love and acceptance. It could not have been written without the support of my family and my family of friends. You have all had my back. I hope I have been there for you in equal measure.

July